God's Tapestry of Time

Book 1

**A Journey Through the Moedim:
Traditional and Messianic Jewish Insights**

Book 2

**Celebrating Tradition Beyond the Torah:
Some Major Non-Biblical Jewish Holidays
Explained**

Terry Brown

Embark on a profound spiritual journey with "God's Tapestry of Time," a captivating two-part exploration into the sacred fabric of the Moedim and beyond.

In Book 1, "A Journey Through the Moedim", discover the intricate weaving of traditional and Messianic Jewish insights, unravelling the divine significance of each Moed. Delve into the rich tapestry of Judaism, where history and faith intertwine to illuminate the sacred path.

Book 2, "Celebrating Tradition Beyond the Torah," unveils the mysteries behind major non-Biblical Jewish holidays. Unearth these celebrations' cultural and spiritual significance, providing a deeper understanding of Jewish heritage.

Written by a Messianic Jew from a church background, this book is a testament to a lifetime of devotion and a call for Christians to embrace the beauty of their shared faith in the Jewish Messiah. Join the author on this enlightening odyssey, where the threads of history, faith, and celebration converge in God's divine masterpiece: His tapestry of time.

© All rights reserved. No part of this book may be reproduced or distributed in any form without prior permission from the author, with the exception of non-commercial uses permitted by copyright law.

God's Tapestry of Time

Book 1
A Journey Through the Moedim: Traditional and Messianic Insights

1.	Introduction.	8
2.	The journey begins.	15
3.	The concept of time	32
4.	An overview of the major festivals	37
5.	Shabbat / Sabbath	40
	a. Shabbat or Lord's Day?	55
6.	Rosh Chodesh / New Month	68
7.	Pesach / Passover	72
8.	HaMatzot / Unleavened bread	85
9.	HaBikkurim / First fruit	88
	a. Sefirat HaOmer / Counting the Omer	94
10.	Shavuot / Pentecost	96
11.	Yom Teruah / Trumpets	102
12.	Yom Kippur / Day of Atonement	108
13.	Sukkot / Tabernacles, Booths	114
	a. Shemini Atzeret	120
	b. Simchat Torah/ Joy of Torah	120
14.	Conclusion - Traditional Jewish perspective	122
15.	Conclusion - Messianic Jewish perspective	125
16.	Messianic Re-cap chart	128

Book 2
Celebrating Tradition Beyond the Torah: Non-Biblical Jewish Holidays Unveiled

1. Introduction — 130
2. An overview of the main events. — 135
3. Asarah B'Tevet / Fast of Tevet. — 138
4. Hannukah /Festival of Light — 142
5. Lag BaOmer - 33rd day of the Omer — 147
6. Purim / feast of lots — 150
7. Tzom Tammuz / Seventeenth of Tammuz — 155
8. Tisha B'Av / Seventeenth of Tammuz — 158
9. Tu Bishvat / New year for the trees — 161
10. Yom HaAliyah / Alyiah day — 167
11. Yom HaShoah/Holocaust Remembrance Day — 171
12. Yom Ha'atzmaut / Israel Independence Day — 176
13. Yom Hazikaron / Memorial Day — 181
14. Yom Yerushalayim / Yerushalayim Day — 185
15. What have we learned? — 189
16. This is only the beginning. — 192

God's Tapestry Of Time.

Preface

The Weaver

My life is but a weaving between my Lord and me.
I cannot choose the colours He worketh steadily.
Oft times He weaveth sorrow, and I, in foolish pride,
Forget He sees the upper, and I the underside.
Not till the loom is silent, and the shuttles cease to fly,
Shall God unroll the canvas and explain the reason why
The dark threads are as needful in the weaver's skillful hand,
As the threads of gold and silver in the pattern He has planned.
He knows. He loves. He cares. Nothing this truth can dim.
He gives His very best to those who leave the choice to Him.

Grant Colfax Tullar

Throughout this book, I will be using some Hebrew names and terms. Here are the main ones. The Hebrew names for the feasts, fasts, and festivals will be given and explained at the start of their respective chapters.

Yeshua = Known by many as Jesus, Yeshua is the Hebrew name given to the Messiah when he was born. It means Salvation.

Torah = The first five books of the Bible.

Shabbat = Sabbath, lasting from sundown on Friday evening until sundown on Saturday.

TaNaKh = The Old Covenant/Testament. This name is derived from the initials of the three categories of writings in what is also known as the Hebrew Scriptures. They are **T**orah (the first five books). **N**evi'im (Prophets) and **K**etuvim (Writings).

Sha'ul = Paul's Hebrew name.

Shofar = A ram's horn blown on special occasions and typically translated in Scripture as 'trumpet.'

Yerushalayim = Jerusalem

Mitzvah = Commandment

Moed / Moedim = God's appointed time/times

Yom = Day

Tzom = Fast

Book 1
A Journey Through the Moedim: Traditional and Messianic Insights

Chapter 1

Introduction

At the core of our existence beats an eternal rhythm, transcending cultural and religious boundaries. This divine cadence celebrates life's sacred seasons and faith's enduring essence. In Judaism, these sacred moments are called "Moedim," signifying appointed times. They hold profound significance for traditional and Messianic Jews, intertwining their spiritual odyssey.

In the intricate tapestry of Jewish tradition, the Moedim are sacred appointments marking pivotal moments in God's calendar. They are not mere rituals but spiritual bridges that connect the Creator with His people. From the solemnity of Yom Kippur to the exuberance of Sukkot, each Moed offers a unique lens through which we can explore our faith, grasp our purpose and look to our future.

This book embarks on a captivating journey through the Moedim, bridging the gap between traditional Judaism and Messianic belief. Together, we unravel the layers of meaning and threads of continuity that weave these ancient observances into the heart of our faith.

Drawing from the depths of Jewish history, we delve into the roots of these appointed times, understanding how they have shaped the collective identity of the Jewish people. Throughout the ages, they have marked waypoints in God's narrative with His chosen people

- a testament to His unchanging character and unwavering commitment.

From the Messianic perspective, we discern a profound connection between the Moedim and the ultimate fulfilment found in Yeshua, the promised Messiah. As Messianic Jews, we stand at the crossroads of ancient tradition and God's redemptive plan through Yeshua HaMashiach - the Messiah. In these appointed times, we discover a tapestry woven with threads of prophecy, fulfilled promises, and the enduring presence of the Divine.

"A Journey through the Moedim: Traditional Jewish and Messianic Insights" invites you on a transformative voyage through the Moedim, where tradition and belief harmonise to unveil the profound mysteries of God's plan for the salvation of His people.

Within these pages, we shall explore the Moedim through the lenses of tradition and faith, embarking on a journey that illuminates the beauty of our shared heritage. The Moedim, as described in the Bible, are a series of divine appointments prescribed by God to mark His calendar. Each Moed is a sacred time for reflection, worship, and renewal, serving as pathways to understanding the intricate relationship between God and His people.

For traditional Jews, the Moedim are cornerstones of their faith, guiding them through the cyclical Jewish year. For Messianic Jews, these appointed times bridge their Jewish heritage with their belief in Yeshua, the Messiah.

The Moedim create a spiritual rhythm, fostering a deep sense of identity, gratitude, and an ongoing relationship with the Almighty, reinforcing the covenantal bond between God and the Jewish people.

Our exploration begins with the weekly Shabbat (Sabbath) and the Rosh Chodesh (New Month) celebrations before journeying through Pesach (Passover), the starting point of the seasons. This ancient festival commemorates the Israelites' liberation from Egyptian bondage.

For traditional Jews, Pesach is a time of remembrance, where they recount their ancestors' exodus from slavery in Egypt and partake in the symbolic Pesach Seder meal. This festival period includes Hamatzah (Unleavened Bread) and HaBikkurim (Firstfruits). Messianic Jews also find profound meaning in Pesach, viewing it as a foreshadowing of Yeshua, the Passover Lamb, who brings ultimate liberation through His death, burial, and resurrection.

From Pesach, our journey continues through the other Moedim: Shavuot (Pentecost), a harvest festival celebrated by traditional Jews, and for Messianic Jews, a remembrance of the giving of the Torah and the outpouring of the Holy Spirit. We explore Yom Teruah, the shofar (trumpet) blowing, and Yom Kippur, the Day of Atonement - moments of reflection and repentance. Finally, Sukkot, the Feast of Tabernacles, emerges as a time of joy and gratitude, embodying the Messianic hope of God dwelling among His people.

One of the most intriguing aspects of this journey is the intersection of tradition and Messianic faith. For Messianic Jews, the Moedim are not just part of their heritage but serve as a bridge connecting their past and their belief in Yeshua as the Messiah. The symbolism within the Moedim gains new depth, reflecting the fulfilment of God's promises in Yeshua's life, death, resurrection and return.

Throughout this exploration, we encounter the harmoniously intertwined melodies of tradition and faith, echoing the profound unity of the Jewish and Messianic journeys. The Moedim stand as a powerful testament to the enduring connection between God and His people, highlighting the divine threads weaving through the tapestry of all our lives.

"A Journey through the Moedim" is an invitation to journey through these sacred seasons and understand their profound significance in the lives of traditional Jews and Messianic Jews alike. Through their rich history, symbolism, and deep spiritual resonance, we embark on a shared journey of faith that brings us closer to the heart of God. It reminds us that, despite our differences, we are bound together during the Moedim seasons.

As we embark on this exploration, let us approach the Moedim with open hearts and eager spirits, ready to uncover the profound truths awaiting us in the appointed times of our faith. Together, let us discover the beauty, depth, and unity at the heart of our shared heritage.

As with any journey, we must start by understanding why it's necessary and what drives us to undertake it. We consider the cost, the route, the stops along the way, and what awaits us at the ultimate destination.

This is a journey we will repeatedly make, revisiting the same stops again and again. Initially, each stop will fill us with curiosity and excitement as we seek to savour the novelty of the experience and extract its full value.

As time goes on and the journey becomes routine, we can easily fall into the habit of simply going through the motions. Each stop may lose some of its initial allure. Therefore, we must continuously reflect on the significance of each stop on the journey, aiming to discover new layers of meaning and potentially overlooked details with each visit.

But unlike when we are the driver on any journey, we are not in control here. We are but the passengers on this divine journey, guided by a higher force. As passengers, we can take our time to observe and contemplate as we travel. We can reflect on our lives at each stop, seeking fresh perspectives and experiencing the moment's beauty with open hearts and willing spirits.

Above all, we must remember who set this journey in motion - the God of Israel, the God of Abraham, Isaac, and Jacob. He designed this journey, placing each stop along the way with unique and specific meanings, from the journey's beginning through each remarkable stop to the glorious destination that awaits those who choose to embark on it.

For some, this journey will be new, full of things to see, learn, and experience. For others, it will be a familiar path, taken many times. However, it's a journey that can always touch us anew when we contemplate its many varied and beautiful facets.

As an example of how we can keep these times fresh, let us consider the Shabbat. In our quest to nurture a life rich in freshness and vibrancy, aligned with God's sacred timings, this stands as a sanctuary in time, a pause in our unending cycles, inviting us to commune with our Creator and marvel at the splendour of His creation.

Intriguingly, this sense of wonder of creation often resonates more profoundly with self-described atheists, whose vocations lead them to expose and magnify the natural world's splendours on our TV screens than it does with the professing believer.

In the whirl of daily existence and the hustle and bustle of life, we may unwittingly overlook many of the wonders surrounding us. Most of us, captivated by televised spectacles, recognise that many of these breathtaking sights and sounds are beyond our reach of experiencing first-hand.

Yet, if we would only allow ourselves the luxury of occasionally meandering through the countryside surrounding us, savouring the sites and sounds, we could quickly and easily lose ourselves in the awe-inspiring diversity of life and the vibrant mosaic of colours and music that nature, as an expression of God's magnificent creation, lavishes upon us each day.

These moedim are like big, colourful pictures that evoke many different feelings and thoughts and will mean different things to different people at various times. They help us learn, feel connected to others, and grow, showing how personal religion can be. For example, Yom Kippur is a solemn day that leads many to reflect deeply on their lives or feel a stronger bond with their community.

On the other hand, Sukkot is a joyful festival where some celebrate by appreciating nature, while others take the opportunity to connect with history. During Pesach, people commonly experience a growth in their faith and cherish time spent with family.

Let's pause, reflect deeply, and immerse ourselves in life's sacred moments' profound beauty and significance. They are not mere dates on a calendar but a testament to the wonder and thoughtfulness of the creator who set them in place. They are rich with meaning, symbolising profound truths, and they guide us towards a greater appreciation of the wonder of the creator's design.

These moments, intricately woven into the tapestry of our existence, hold meaning, give direction, and reflect something much more significant than ourselves. By embracing a fresh perspective and a genuine desire to understand them more fully, we can uncover the deeper essence of what these times represent and how they connect us to the grand tapestry of life.

This journey of discovery is not just about gaining knowledge but about enriching our spirits and drawing us closer to the profound beauty woven into our existence by our amazing Creator God.

Embarking on the "Journey Through The Moedim" is an invitation to engage deeply with the profound rhythms and teachings embedded in these sacred times. It is a call to approach these

Even after carefully considering these factors, I experienced a sense of calm when I decided to leave the church and embrace Messianic Judaism.

My journey within the church had spanned over three decades, encompassing two years of full-time study at an Anglican Theological College, a decade of full-time Christian ministry, and almost two years serving as a church minister in London. (You can find a more detailed explanation of the reasons for this transition in my earlier book, "That was Then. This is Now," available from Amazon.co.uk).

Nevertheless, the driving force behind this shift can be briefly explained by some notable disparities between my interpretation and growing understanding of Scripture and certain long-held and cherished church doctrines. These disparities, small and few though they may have seemed to some, were too significant for me to overlook or ignore.

In my previous book, I emphasised that my issues did not include that of salvation. Salvation comes through faith alone, a fundamental truth I share with my brothers and sisters in the Christian church who know and love the Lord.

However, the challenge I encountered was simply a desire to be obedient to all of God's Word - including the teachings that many, including myself in the past, dismissed as irrelevant or not binding to contemporary believers.

Yeshua explicitly told us we had to live by every word of God, and there lay the root of my disquiet. The word 'every' does not allow us the luxury of omitting, ignoring or changing anything in God's word to suit ourselves and certainly not if, by doing so, they cause a conflict with any other parts of God's Word.

Messianic Judaism taught me how living with every single word of God was possible.

So when I first embraced Messianic Judaism, and without needing to relocate to another country, I was confident the transition would be relatively smooth. My reasoning was straightforward: I wouldn't need to acquire a new language (although gaining some basic knowledge of Hebrew terms could be beneficial).

Messianic Judaism and my previous Christian faith embraced the Old Covenant, the Old Testament or the Hebrew Bible. Having already attained a reasonably solid grasp of the New Covenant, I entered this new phase of my spiritual journey, not expecting to need to acquire much additional knowledge. While this mindset may verge on arrogance, conversations with others who have navigated a similar path have shown me that I am not the only one who thought like this at that juncture.

It turns out my initial assumptions were entirely inaccurate. I believed that my familiarity with the Bible was sufficient for a long-standing member of the Church like me to make this transition almost effortlessly. But as it happened, I couldn't have been more mistaken.

I soon realised that there were significant portions of Scripture, including some of the teachings of Yeshua and Sha'ul in the New Testament, that I had misinterpreted, misunderstood or, to my surprise, completely overlooked. It was evident that God did not provide us with His Word so that we could selectively disregard parts of it or treat it like a pick-and-mix buffet.

My earnest desire was to truly understand and adhere to it correctly. All of it. Every word, just as Yeshua commanded. Please remember that when Yeshua said 'every word of Scripture,' the only Scripture in existence at that time was the Hebrew Scriptures, what most believers call the Old Testament.

So, that's what He was commanding me to do. To follow every word, every commandment, of the Old Testament, and although I believed I was being obedient, that was not something I could claim, in all honesty, to be doing.

It turned out that my knowledge was somewhat limited concerning some portions of the Old Testament Scriptures, especially the section that we incorrectly label as the 'law', which discusses, among other things, what are known as the feasts, fasts, and festivals. These are found in the Torah, the initial five books of the Old Covenant, Genesis, Exodus, Leviticus, Numbers and Deuteronomy, which cover all the commandments God gave us.

In the past, I had not shown the feasts, or many of the other commandments, much consideration because I had unquestioningly accepted the teachings I had received, which asserted that these practices were solely intended for the Jewish community and held little or no significance for the church.

However, after delving into a more comprehensive study, I realised that no biblical foundation existed to support this viewpoint.

The festivals, God's appointed times or Moedim, are integral to the Torah, the Bible's first five books, which the church labels as 'law'. Despite assertions by most people in the church that the law has been abolished or changed and are no longer in effect, this contradicts the teachings of Yeshua, as conveyed in Matthew 5:17-19. He said he did not come to abolish the law nor change even the smallest part of it, and to take any other line than this is undoubtedly to be disobedient at best or to insinuate Yeshua lied at worst. If it's the latter, it disqualifies him from being the sinless Saviour.

Let's delve into the law's role in the New Covenant, as outlined in Jeremiah 31:33. This passage speaks of a time when God's laws, the "Torah" in Hebrew, will be internalised and written on our hearts. This idea tells us categorically, that the Torah remains central, and should be ingrained within us under the New Covenant.

The notion that the Torah might be nullified or abolished by the crucifixion is contradictory to this concept, and the words of Yeshua. There's no indication in Scripture of any alternative laws replacing the Torah. There can be no doubt that Yeshua himself affirmed that every aspect of the Torah, even the most minor details, would remain valid.

To underscore this, 1 John 3:4 describes sin as 'transgression of the law,' referring explicitly to "the Torah." If the law were abolished, there would be nothing to transgress, effectively eradicating the possibility of sinning and negating the need for a saviour.

However, this idea conflicts with Scripture's consistent message that everyone has sinned. That means everybody has transgresed the Torah - broken the 'law'.

To say the Torah has been abolished is like removing all speed limits and then attempting to penalise a driver for speeding. The analogy illustrates the necessity of the Torah still being in effect and how we must adhere to it. (How this is possible is covered in my previously mentioned book).

At this point, many claim it's legalism, trying to earn salvation by keeping the law rather than accepting salvation by faith.

But Yeshua answered this accusation of legalism when he continued explaining in Matthew 5 that those who keep the law and teach others to keep it and those who don't keep it and teach others not to keep it both get into the Kingdom. Both are saved, the obedient and the disobedient. Only their position in the Kingdom is different.

One of the greatest deceptions among believers today is that faith has replaced obedience. This is not a salvation issue or one of faith, but one of obedience. Keeping the law, the Torah, therefore, must include following the commandments, and that applies to those concerning the Moedim, God's appointed times.

I know some churches occasionally organise what they refer to as a Passover meal. However, it seems many do so more out of curiosity and personal interest rather than as strict adherence to God's teachings.

Suppose the intention is to be genuinely obedient to God's Word. In that case, one might question why this particular festival is the only one selected to be observed while neglecting the others that are equally commanded to be kept.

Faithful obedience to God's Word implies not cherry-picking which parts to observe based on personal preferences but embracing the entirety of His commandments. We are called to obey all His teachings, and no alternatives are provided or allowed.

In addition to the Shabbat (Sabbath) and Rosh Chodesh (the new month), the Torah lists seven Moedim, God's appointed times, and we are commanded in Scripture to observe all of them. God does not give them as suggestions or recommendations. They are commandments for all who want to be more fully obedient to God's Word.

In addition to the Scripturally commanded Moedim, there are many other feasts, fasts, festivals, and special days celebrated and commemorated by Jews worldwide that aren't recorded in Scripture. While God does not command us to keep these other times, they often mark some significant event in the history of God's people and can contain valuable lessons for all of us.

For example, because of its historical significance, the Scriptures tell us that Yeshua and his disciples observed and celebrated Hanukkah, often called the festival of lights or dedication in some translations, even though it's not a commandment of God. If

Yeshua and his disciples felt it was worth observing, shouldn't we? (John 10:22).

If we are to be imitators of Him, surely that means doing what He did, teaching what He taught and following His example. If there is nothing for us to gain from them, why did God include them in his word? Everything in Scripture is there for a reason if we just look for it. These appointed times have a vital message for us today if we only knew how to interpret them and understand what they mean.

Unlike the Moedim outlined in Scripture that God has commanded us to observe, the Christian Church recognises two primary celebrations: Christmas and Easter. It's worth noting that God ordains neither of these occasions, and they certainly don't have any specific directives in the Scriptures. The big question is, do they conflict with the Word of God?

Although the Bible mentions Yeshua's birth, death, and resurrection, there is no Scriptural mandate to commemorate these events through the observance of Christmas or Easter, and it's important to clarify that Scripture does not suggest celebrating Christmas or Easter as a substitute or alternatives for the appointed times, the Moedim.

For many years, as a church member, I regarded these two celebrations ordained by humans as satisfactory and permissible. Little did I know about their pagan roots or that Scripture had already guided us on when and how we should observe the significance of these momentous occasions—the birth, death, and resurrection of our Saviour, Yeshua.

Scripture clearly outlines God's appointed timing for these events and offers insights into the appropriate manner of commemorating them. In contrast, the church advises us on a different schedule and approach, influenced not by Scripture but by human thoughts and traditions.

Furthermore, the church has also established its designated day for rest and worship: Sunday, often known as the Lord's Day. Believers engage in work during the week and reserve Sunday for attending church, considering it their day of rest and worship.

However, the question arises: is this day ordained by God in the scriptures, or does it go against God's original commands? Is it God's way or man's way? What is the appropriate approach to observing the Shabbat on the seventh day, Saturday?

Interestingly, there is no Scriptural indication that we should abstain from observing the Scriptural definition of the Shabbat. Clarity can be found in the Scriptures if we look closer, more honestly and with a mind open to God's guidance and put that above man's tradition.

Like Judaism, the church likewise observes many additional days in its calendar, each with its unique celebration, albeit with slight variations among different denominations. It is worth contemplating whether these days hold a divine significance and convey any specific message or lesson.

Both faiths' extra commemorative occasions should be examined thoughtfully to discern their alignment with God's teachings, the messages they carry, and whether their lessons can enrich our spiritual journey or possibly detract from it.

Shortly after my conversion to Messianic Judaism, I came to a crossroads on my faith journey: to follow God's laws as outlined in the Torah and echoed by Yeshua or to adhere to human traditions.

I finally and entirely accepted that I needed to let go of the traditions not rooted in Scripture and which were holding me back. Trying to keep a foot in both camps would only compromise my complete obedience to God's Scriptural commandments.

However, despite being fully supported by Scripture, my decision was rejected by many in my church community, resulting in the loss of some cherished friendships.

Nonetheless, I stood firm in my conviction, choosing to follow God's commands over preserving those relationships, no matter how meaningful they were to me.

As I delved deeper into studying God's word with a more open and attentive mindset, I gradually saw that these were unmistakably not the feasts and festivals of only the Jewish tradition, as I had previously been told and firmly believed. The Scriptures provide the evidence for this.

*Leviticus 23:2. Speak to the Israelites and say to them: "These are **my** appointed festivals, the appointed festivals **of the Lord**,"*
*Leviticus 23:4 "These are the **Lord's** appointed festivals,"*
*Leviticus 23:37 "These are the **Lord's** appointed festivals,"*

Four times in that one chapter, God repeated that these are His, God's, appointed times. They are not Jewish. They are not man's. They are God's.

When God communicates a message, it's essential to pay attention. If He emphasises the same point repeatedly, it becomes even more critical to heed His words. In this chapter, God has stressed four times that these appointed festivals belong to Him, which should be enough to gain our full attention.

Despite this, I still retained, as we all do, the ability to make my own decisions, thanks to the free will God has granted me. The decision was to choose between God's or man's paths. It has to be one way or the other. There is no middle way. Although we all have the freedom to choose, the choice was obvious and straightforward for me, what we would call today a no-brainer.

These Moedim are times God has set apart for us to meet with him in celebration, commemoration, and remembrance. God tells us these are **_His_** appointed times. Times that He has called us to keep and set apart to do what He says and for us to come into His presence.

We don't do it to earn favour in His eyes. It's done purely out of obedience, our love for Him, and our desire to please Him. You don't have to go far through the Gospels to see that Yeshua, His disciples, the Apostles, and the early believers kept all these appointed times.

There is nowhere in the New Covenant, either in the Gospels or in the letters, that it tells us that these appointed times have been removed or replaced or that we can ignore them. And it certainly doesn't mean we can change them to do what we want. God's Word doesn't even hint at any of these things. It is just the opposite. They are for all believers, and they are to be kept.

Several references in both the Gospels and the NT letters indicate that we should be keeping these appointed times.

Matthew 26:17-20, Mark 14:12-16, and Luke 22:7-16 show that Yeshua and his followers observed Pesach, the Passover.

Luke 22:1 refers to the feast of HaMatzah, unleavened bread, part of the Pesach period, when Yeshua's enemies plotted to kill Him, knowing He would be in Yerushalayim observing it, just as God commanded.

In John 7:2-10, Yeshua went to Yerushalayim to keep the feast of Tabernacles (also known as the feast of Booths) in accordance with and in obedience to the Scriptures.

Acts 21:20 On hearing it, they praised God, but they also said to him, *"You see, brother, how many tens of thousands of believers there are among the Jews, and they are all zealous for the Torah.*

Zealous for the Torah meant that they followed and obeyed all of God's commandments in the Bible's first five books.

It shows without any doubt whatsoever that Yeshua, His disciples, and the early believers were faithful followers of God's instructions to observe these God-ordained celebrations. Yeshua never indicated they would end when he left or that anyone had the authority to replace them with something different - just the opposite.

Sha'ul tells us that we should be imitators of him as he is an imitator of Yeshua. To be an imitator means to do as they do, so if we are to imitate Yeshua, we are called to follow God's full instructions just as Yeshua did, just as the disciples and apostles did, and just as Sha'ul did.

While Sha'ul acknowledges the significance of God's festivals, he also emphasises the spiritual truths they point to and their fulfilment in Yeshua, the Messiah. By ignoring them, we are not only being disobedient to God's commands but also risk missing or misunderstanding these vital spiritual truths.

The Moedim, God's appointed times, which I cover in Book 1, hold significant religious and historical importance for Jewish people from all streams of Judaism and are observed yearly. But they also hold profound spiritual truth for all believers by commemorating historical events that foreshadow our ultimate future.

Each festival has distinct themes and rituals, collectively contributing to the rhythm of Jewish life and fostering a sense of community, spirituality, and cultural identity.

The Moedim provide a framework for retelling the story of the Jewish people's journey from slavery to freedom, the giving of the Torah at Mount Sinai, and the providence of God throughout history. They also emphasise concepts such as gratitude, repentance, renewal, and ethical behaviour.

Collectively, the Moedim are sacred opportunities for connecting with God. They play a central role in much of Jewish tradition, serving to remember, celebrate, and transmit core beliefs and values from one generation to the next. Observing the Moedim involves a mix of various rituals, prayers, traditions, and customs that help Jews deepen their understanding of their faith and relationship with God.

For example, during Passover, Jews retell the story of the Exodus, consume unleavened bread (matzah), and participate in a Seder meal. During Sukkot, temporary shelters are constructed to remind them of the Israelites' journey through the wilderness, and during Shavuot, the giving of the Torah is celebrated through study and prayer.

The Moedim emphasises themes like freedom (Passover), gratitude for the harvest (First fruit) and learning (Shavuot), self-reflection and repentance (Yom Teruah and Yom Kippur), and the impermanence of life here (Sukkot).

Together, they create a cyclical rhythm in time that helps Jewish individuals and communities maintain a solid connection to their faith, values, and shared history. The overall conclusion that can be drawn from the Moedim is the significance of remembrance, renewal, connection with historical events and spiritual teachings.

While it is accepted that all of these things apply to those within traditional Judaism, Scripture makes it quite clear that they are relevant to all believers. There is nowhere we are told that there is one teaching for Jews and one for non-Jews. We have one God, one Saviour and one Scripture.

We are all one family with the same Father, whether we are of natural birth or adopted. Adopted children have the same rights as natural ones. And just as we have the same rights, we also have the same obligations. We can't have one without the other.

It's important to note that interpretations and practices can vary among Jewish traditions (Orthodox, Conservative, Reform, Messianic, etc.). Variations can also be found within local congregations and individuals.

However, whatever differences there are, observing these Moedim is considered a sacred and vital part of those born into the Jewish faith and for those who are adopted into the family - those 'grafted in'.

While different branches of Judaism, including Messianic Judaism, may have varying perspectives on the appointed times, you will see that there are many commonalities across these branches, particularly in the way the festivals are celebrated and the traditions and foods connected with them.

You will witness a deep intertwining of history, spirituality, the cyclical nature of God's calendar, and the sense of continuity, remembrance, and anticipation for the future it brings.

The Moedim are observed with special prayers, rituals, festive meals, and customs that may vary slightly depending on the holiday and the Jewish community. But these festivals are essential in connecting individuals to God's people's history, values, and community. You will see what they are, what they commemorate, what they point to, how they're celebrated, and many associated traditions.

You may then start to appreciate, just as I did, why God gave the Moedim to us and how much richer our lives of faith will become when we are more fully obedient to His Word by observing them.

Regarding timelines, these events, which mark the regular passing of the seasons, will give you an appreciation of the past events to help enrich your present faith and reveal the fantastic future awaiting you.

Along with the traditional Jewish view comes a Messianic perspective that recognises historical milestones and significant past events which anticipate and point to the coming of the Messiah and the eventual redemption of the world.

We will delve into these appointed times more closely, exploring how they are observed and celebrated across Jewish communities. This brief examination will include many unique traditions tied to each occasion and the practices that define them.

We will look into how these times are commemorated by various branches of Judaism, including those who identify with Messianic Judaism. By doing so, we aim to provide a rich and nuanced understanding of the multifaceted ways these important times are honoured and experienced within the Jewish faith.

Messianic Judaism represents a resurgent and rapidly expanding movement rooted in the early first century. It harmoniously melds the principles of first-century Judaism with a profound belief in Yeshua as the Messiah, remaining firmly entrenched in his practised traditions.

It is crucial to emphasise that Messianic Judaism stands apart from conventional Christianity and is not a mere hybrid of Judaism and Christianity. Instead, it constitutes a faith firmly grounded in the Torah and centred on Yeshua, affirming devotion to the one true God of Israel.

This brand of Judaism can trace its lineage back to the teachings and practices of Yeshua, his disciples, and the apostles, predating the establishment of the Christian Church by many decades. Its origins are deeply intertwined with the Jewish traditions that Yeshua, his predecessors, and prior generations adhered to and observed.

It's noteworthy that neither the Gospels nor the epistles of the New Covenant contain any suggestion that Yeshua came to initiate a new religious movement called Christianity or institute a distinct gathering place called the church. To ascertain the accuracy of this assertion, one only needs to read the New Covenant with an open mind, look into the original language in which it was composed, and at the Jewish culture of the day.

Yeshua, as a devout first-century Jew, diligently adhered to the Torah. He dedicated himself to proclaiming and teaching its precepts and attended the Synagogue every Sabbath. Consequently, he faithfully observed all the Moedim, the divinely appointed times. He dutifully fulfilled the Mitzvot, the commandments that applied to him as a Jewish male.

Scripture provides few details on the specific ways to celebrate and remember the Moedim, focusing mainly on the importance of simply observing them, often without giving detailed instructions. This has led to the development of numerous traditions surrounding these festivals, shaped by centuries of practice. As a result, how the Moedim are celebrated can vary significantly among different Jewish individuals, communities, and cultures.

However, it's essential to approach these traditions with discernment and caution. The sparse instructions in Scripture mean there's a danger for traditions to overshadow the original intent of the Moedim. Over time, the focus can shift from following God's word to prioritising human customs.

While these traditions aren't necessarily bad, it's essential to remember that the core purpose is observing these times as commanded by God. This purpose goes beyond just enjoyment, although enjoying these celebrations is perfectly acceptable when done in the right spirit.

These are moments when we are called to pause and spend time with God, expressing gratitude for all He has accomplished, commemorating His miraculous deeds, and anticipating our glorious future. However, when traditions begin to overshadow this purpose, it is essential to exercise great caution. Traditions should not supersede God's Word.

Book One is written to give more information concerning these God-ordained appointed times for the newcomer to Messianic Judaism. It's an introductory exploration rather than an exhaustive dissertation on the Moedim.

It provides a fundamental overview of their essence, significance in commemorating specific events, and the profound messages they convey through their symbolism.

Additionally, it delves into the rich tapestry of customs, rituals, traditions, and often the culinary delights associated with these occasions, offering insights from both traditional and Messianic Jewish perspectives.

So, this work is tailored for individuals new to the Messianic Jewish faith or those within the broader church community who are curious about God's divinely appointed times. It provides a tantalising glimpse into this sacred realm, with the sincere aspiration of kindling the reader's curiosity to explore the Moedim deeper.

The hope is that readers will be inspired to study these divine appointments further, expanding their understanding and appreciation.

Alongside these divinely ordained Moedim, the Jewish faith encompasses a multitude of other feasts, festivals, and special observances, each holding its significance.

In Book Two, I have included details of the most commonly celebrated of these so that the two books combined may be used as a reference work to help newcomers to Messianic Judaism, or the curious within the church, become more familiar with the beauty and fullness of the Jewish faith.

May you be richly blessed in your studies and how you implement and practise what you discover.

"Study is not the most important thing, but action. Study is not the goal; rather, study leads to action." - Rabbi Tarfon (Pirkei Avot 2:15)

Chapter 3.

The Concept of Time

"Time," said Albert Einstein, "is what prevents everything from happening at once."

It is something that very few of us spend any of thinking about. However, although we often refer to it in our everyday conversations, I suspect many of us would find it difficult to define what time is.

Suppose we were of a very organised mind. In that case, we might come up with something like, 'Time can be defined as a continuous progression of moments or intervals that separate past, present, and future. It provides a framework for organising and understanding the order and duration of events.'

Or were we of a more scientific mindset, it might go something like, "The scientific concept of time encompasses a range of theories and perspectives, from the classical view of time as an absolute and independent quantity to the relativistic and quantum descriptions that consider time as a dynamic and interconnected dimension."

Well, that goes beyond my limits of sound comprehension, so perhaps a more everyday description, and one more closely aligned to my thinking, would go more like, 'It is something we live in. We have lived through our past and are yet to live in our future. So we are currently living in the present.'

But in our everyday existence, we rarely take the time to try to explain it. We usually only reference it briefly in passing, and those references typically come in one of three different forms.

Firstly, we can use a linear description to talk about marking the passing of time. The thinking is clear. There is a starting point and a line tracking time from that point until - well, we can be somewhat vague here. We will inevitably differ somewhat in how, where, and when we see that line coming to an end.

We visualise time as a long, straight line running from start to finish. Etched out on this line, we see the marking of the years at regular intervals, and we have the beginning and end of the numerous events, ages, and eras defined on this line.

Some will be a one-time mark, such as depicting the birth or death of a person. Others will have a start and finish shown on the line, such as the reign of various monarchs and kingdoms or the conflicts that have blighted our history, such as the two World Wars of the 20th century.

Secondly, we have a more cyclical description of time, where we will likely use phrases such as, "It's that time again" or "Has it come around already?"

It could be a reference to the new year starting, another birthday being notched up, or, for the more sporting-minded of us, it can be the passing of the four years waiting for the World Cup or the Olympics to come around again, or perhaps the annual Wimbledon tennis championship.

This cyclical view of time sees regular events happening repeatedly for whatever period it may last. Naturally, the repeating of our birthdays only occurs until our demise. Other events, such as the marking of the annual seasons, can be traced over millennia.

Finally, there is the psychological aspect of time. This is how we perceive its passing. There is a line in a Moody Blues song (for those of us with enough birthday 'cycles' under our belts to remember the 1960s) that states, "Time seems to stand quite still. In a child's world, it always will."

Children give little or no thought to the passing of time, except perhaps counting the days until a special occasion they are particularly excited about, such as a birthday party, a trip to a fun park, school holidays, etc.

Conversely, how often have we heard, or even said ourselves, that time seems to fly as we get older? Hardly one week has started before we are at the weekend and then getting ready to begin the next one. Time flies, as the saying goes.

Sitting through a long, boring speech can seem like an age, even though it may only be half an hour. On the other hand, if we are enjoying something, it appears it has hardly started before it's finished. On those occasions, several hours can fly by in what seems like no time at all. In reality, time passes at the same pace in both events. We just feel that it's either dragged on or flown by.

The famous author and Theologian C.S. Lewis reminds us, *"The future is something which everyone reaches at the rate of 60 minutes an hour, whatever he does, whoever he is."*

The truth is that all three of these descriptions often come into play simultaneously. The linear tapestry of time is constantly woven with many events, beginning at the starting point and working steadily towards the end, while simultaneously, the various-sized wheels of cyclical time roll along the tapestry, repeatedly stamping their markings as they go.

Days of the week, months of the year, and numerous other events are all marked in regular patterns over and over as the wheels of time roll around. And that is how we generally mark the passing of time. The seconds, minutes, hours, days, weeks, years, decades, and generations are our way of recording the passing of time.

We have our schedules, timetables, and deadlines to keep to, and we closely tie time to our idea of progress and productivity, emphasising accomplishing tasks, meeting deadlines, and achieving goals within specific timeframes. Relating our lives to time influences many aspects of our lives.

Yes, we have our own timetables, individual and corporate, but God also has a timetable that He has given us. He has laid out for us the occasions when we are called to take note and act on His calendar of passing time. He has placed the marks on His rolling time wheel. As it progresses cyclically along the tapestry of time, they notate His timetable at regular intervals.

He has told us that these are His occasions and the events that He wants us to remember, commemorate, and celebrate. He has commanded us clearly in His Word the what, when, and often the how of keeping them.

Indeed, there is nothing wrong with remembering and celebrating other historical events in our lives. There is ample room to mark the rolling around and marking of our cyclical wheels on this rich tapestry of time. Birthdays, anniversaries, etc. It is good to do so; there is nowhere in God's Word that He has told us he doesn't want us to do that.

But by the same token, He has commanded, not recommended, asked, or suggested that we follow His instructions to remember and keep His events that His wheel stamps out on each full rotation. And clearly, the wheels of our time should be secondary in our lives to His.

God's calendar is often called the Jewish calendar, not because it is theirs alone but because it was to the Jewish people that he entrusted it, in the same way that He entrusted them to preserve the Scriptures of the Tanakh (the Old Testament). It is a task they fought long and hard to achieve successfully, and for which we should all be extremely grateful.

God's calendar reflects a rich blend of historical events and religious observances. It follows a unique calendar that combines lunar and solar calculations. It outlines a rich and wide variety of holidays and festivals throughout the year, which mark significant historical events, tell of the future they point to, and provide us with opportunities for reflection, commemoration, celebration, and anticipation.

Book 1 begins with a brief description of the Moedim - the sacred appointments, or divinely ordained times, that the narrative will explore. Initially, each Scriptural ordained observance is introduced concisely, providing a foundational understanding for readers.

As the book progresses, we will delve deeper into the significance and intricacies of each Moedim through individual chapters dedicated to them. Within these chapters, you will discover a more comprehensive and detailed examination, sharing insights and reflections inspired by divine guidance.

In this, you will find profound blessings in celebrating these sacred times, particularly when you can observe them in the company of others. This communal aspect of celebration can enrich your experience and understanding, drawing you closer to the essence of what these appointed times represent.

You are encouraged to approach this journey with an open heart and mind, giving each Moedim the thoughtful consideration it deserves. Reflect on the deeper meanings and messages that these divine appointments hold. Through this exploration, you will discern what God is communicating through these sacred times. Celebrating the Moedim is an act of obedience and a pathway to deeper spiritual insight and connection with the divine.

May you be abundantly blessed in this sacred endeavour, discovering the richness and depth of God's appointed times.

Chapter 4.

An Overview

Before going into detail on each festival, let's go through the list of the Holy Days and Moedim commanded in Scripture, briefly describing each of them. They are all to be found commanded in Scripture.

Shabbat (Sabbath):
- Biblical Origin: The observance of the Shabbat is established in the Book of Genesis (Genesis 2:2-3) when God rested on the seventh day of creation. It's a weekly day of rest, worship, prayer and study that starts Friday evening and ends Saturday evening.

Rosh Chodesh (New Month)
- Biblical Origin: The observance of Rosh Chodesh is based on the biblical commandment to "blow the trumpets" on the first day of each month (Numbers 10:10). The concept of marking the new moon can also be found in the Psalms and other parts of the Hebrew Bible (Old Testament).

Passover (Pesach):
- Biblical Origin: Passover commemorates the Israelites' liberation from slavery in Egypt. Its biblical origin is found in the Book of Exodus (Exodus 12), where God instructed the Israelites to sacrifice a lamb and mark their doorposts with its blood.

Unleavened Bread (Chag HaMatzot):
- Biblical Origin: This feast immediately follows Passover, and its origins are also found in Exodus (Exodus 12:15-20). During this time, leaven (yeast) is removed from Jewish households to symbolise the haste with which the Israelites left Egypt.

Firstfruits (Yom HaBikkurim):
- Biblical Origin: This feast is mentioned in Leviticus 23:9-14. It involves offering the first sheaf of the barley harvest to God, recognising Him as the provider of sustenance.

Pentecost (Shavuot):
- Biblical Origin: Shavuot is found in Leviticus 23:15-22. It's the Festival of Weeks and commemorates the giving of the Torah on Mount Sinai. It is also associated with the first fruits of the wheat harvest.

Trumpets (Yom Teruah):
- Biblical Origin: The Feast of Trumpets is described in Leviticus 23:23-25. While many in Judaism celebrate this as the New Year (Rosh Hashanah), Scripture tells us the first month of God's year is just before Passover, in the month of Nisan (Exodus 12:2).

Atonement (Yom Kippur):
- Biblical Origin: Yom Kippur is outlined in Leviticus 16. It is a day of fasting and reflection, during which the high priest would enter the Holy of

Holies in the Tabernacle or Temple to make atonement for the people's sins.

Tabernacles (Sukkot):
- Biblical Origin: Sukkot is detailed in Leviticus 23:33-43. It commemorates the Israelites' journey through the wilderness. It involves the construction of temporary shelters (a sukkah) to live in during the festival.

Many other holidays in the Jewish calendar are not mentioned here as they are traditional rather than Scriptural. Some are celebrated by those living in the land of Israel, and some for those living in the Diaspora (outside of Israel). Many are for both.

The list of all the dates on which something is commemorated and celebrated within Judaism is quite extensive, numbering around a hundred or so. It is not within the scope of this book to list and explain all of them.

Those non-Scriptural celebrations and commemorations included in Book Two are generally acknowledged and are followed to some degree by most Jewish communities worldwide. These are covered in varying detail according to the traditional manner they are followed. They are outlined as a reference to help guide the newcomer to Messianic Judaism through what initially may seem a confusing plethora of events.

It should always be noted that traditions and customs vary, sometimes significantly, among all forms of Judaism and Jewish communities, including Messianic Judaism and individuals.

Chapter 5.

Shabbat - Take 5, or rather, 25.

"More than Israel has kept the Shabbat,
the Shabbat has kept Israel."   Ahad Ha'am

First, it's worth mentioning that there are additional Shabbatot (plural) connected to the Jewish festivals and feasts that occur throughout the Jewish calendar year in addition to the weekly Shabbat. These Shabbatot are observed in conjunction with specific holidays and observances.

1. Pesach: The first and last days of the seven-day Pesach festival are observed as a Shabbat.
2. Shavuot: The festival of Shavuot is observed as a Shabbat.
3. Yom Teruah: The Feast of Trumpets is observed as a Shabbat. It is a two-day holiday that marks the beginning of the High Holy Days.
4. Yom Kippur: Also known as The Day of Atonement, it is the holiest day in the Jewish calendar. It is observed as a Shabbat and is a day of fasting, prayer and reflection.
5. Sukkot: The first and eighth days of the festival of Sukkot are observed as a Shabbat.

These are the additional Shabbatot observed in Judaism. It's also important to note that the Jewish calendar is lunar-based. Hence, the dates of the festival observances vary yearly on the Gregorian calendar while remaining within their set season. But for now, let's concentrate on the weekly Shabbat.

"Thus the heavens and the earth were finished. And on the seventh day, God finished His work that he had done, and he rested on the seventh day from all his work that he had done. So God blessed the

seventh day and made it holy because on it God rested from all his work that he had done." Genesis 2:1-3

We read how God finished creating everything and rested. Then He declared the seventh day as Holy. To state that anything is Holy is something that only God can do, no matter what any man may say to the contrary. God tells us that we are to remember it is the day He has declared holy; we are to rest from all our work and set the day apart for Him.

This Genesis creation narrative takes place long before any people were known by the names Israelites, Hebrews, or Jews. In addition to this, Yeshua said that Shabbat was made for man. It was not just for the Jews. That means that the Shabbat commandment was for all humanity in the same manner as God's promise not to destroy the world by flood in the days of Noah was.

Then we come to several Scriptural references in the Torah that pertain to the observance of the Shabbat, the day that God declared holy. Here are a few prominent ones:

*Remember the Shabbat day by setting it apart as holy. Six days you are to serve and do all your regular work, but the seventh day shall be a Shabbat rest to the L*ord *your God. Do not do any regular work, neither you, nor your sons or daughters, nor your male or female servants, nor your cattle, nor the alien who is residing inside your gates, for in six days the L*ord *made the heavens and the earth, the sea, and everything that is in them, but he rested on the seventh day. In this way, the L*ord *blessed the seventh day and made it holy.* Exodus 20:8-11

*The L*ord *spoke to Moses. He said, "Speak to the people of Israel. Tell them, 'You must observe my Shabbats diligently because the*

*Shabbat is a sign between me and you throughout your generations, so that you may know that I am the L*ORD*, who sets you apart as holy. So you shall observe the Shabbat, for it is holy to you. Everyone who profanes it must certainly be put to death, for if anyone does any work on the Shabbat, his life shall be cut off from among his people. Work may be done on six days, but the seventh day is a Shabbat of complete rest, holy to the L*ORD*. Whoever does any work on the Shabbat day must be put to death. Therefore, the people of Israel shall observe the Shabbat by keeping the Shabbat throughout their generations as a perpetual covenant. It is a permanent sign between me and the people of Israel, for in six days the L*ORD* made heaven and earth, and on the seventh day he rested and was refreshed.'"* Exodus 31:12-17

*On six days, work may be done, but on the seventh day, there shall be a Shabbat of complete rest, a holy convocation. You shall not do any work. It shall be a Shabbat to the L*ORD* everywhere you live.* Leviticus 23:3

*Observe the Shabbat day by setting it apart as holy, just as the L*ORD* your God commanded you. Six days you are to serve and perform all of your regular work, but the seventh day is a Shabbat rest to the L*ORD* your God. You are not to do any regular work, you or your son or your daughter or your male servant or your female servant or your ox or your donkey or any of your livestock or the alien who resides inside your gates, so that your male servant and your female servant may rest like you. Remember that you were slaves in the land of Egypt and that the L*ORD* your God brought you out from there with a strong hand and an outstretched arm. Therefore the L*ORD* your God commanded you to keep the day of rest.* Deuteronomy 5:12-25

These verses serve as foundational references for the observance of the Shabbat, emphasising the importance of resting on the seventh day, refraining from everyday work, and setting it aside as a day for the Lord. It highlights the importance of sanctification and dedication to God on the seventh day of the week.

But it doesn't just mean we rest and do as little as possible. I'm sorry to disappoint anyone, but slobbing out in our PJs all day on the sofa doesn't cut it. It doesn't just mean stopping usual tasks and switching off totally. God didn't stop work on the seventh day. If He had, all of His creation would have ceased being. What He ceased from was his work of creation. So what does He require of us on Shabbat?

His purpose for creating us is to have a relationship and commune with Him. To help facilitate this, He designated the seventh day for us to pause from our regular activities and devote that time exclusively to Him, to concentrate on and be in His presence.

Our existence is fundamentally about connecting with Him, which is His desire and longing. Therefore, once a week on the Sabbath, He has established a pattern for us to follow. He created the universe in six days and rested on the seventh day from His work of creation, commanding us to do the same to enjoy uninterrupted time with Him, recharging our physical and spiritual batteries before resuming our routine duties.

This doesn't imply that we disregard Him or His teachings during the rest of the week. Instead, it means that while we focus on our daily work for six days, we should completely dedicate one specific day each week to nurture our relationship with Him. This is the day He has chosen for us. He designated the seventh day, the Shabbat, and made it Holy, and there is nowhere in the whole of Scripture that we are told that He has changed it.

The Shabbat always begins at sundown on Friday evening and ends at sunset on Saturday. This timing of the Shabbat, and indeed for every day, comes from the Scriptural account of creation, where we are informed:

There was evening, and there was morning - the first day. Genesis 1:3

God's Word recorded it in that order, so clearly, the day, the period of 24 hours, starts in the evening and runs to the following evening.

However, in Judaism, an hour is generally added to the duration of the Shabbat to prevent any chance that we inadvertently bring the Shabbat to a premature end. That makes the traditional Shabbat observance 25 hours rather than 24.

Although there is very little said in Scripture on how we keep the Shabbat, other than ceasing from our everyday work, there are a great many traditions that have become associated with keeping it. Refraining from work is something that all concur with. However, what defines work has been widely debated.

The most common restrictions today are based on the principles of the Torah, which have been interpreted and expanded by Jewish scholars throughout history. These were based on the prohibited work for constructing and working on the Tabernacle during the Israelites' time in the wilderness and are listed in 39 categories.

While these 39 categories of work are traditionally prohibited on Shabbat, it is essential to note that the specific applications and interpretations will vary among different Jewish communities. Here are the 39 categories of work, known as the "Melachot," considered prohibited on Shabbat. For some people, it will make for fascinating reading. For others, they may seem beyond the understanding of what they are, what they mean and how we are meant to relate to them today.

1. Sowing (Zore's) - Planting or farming.
2. Ploughing (Choreish) - Preparing soil for planting.
3. Reaping (Kotzer) - harvesting crops.
4. Binding sheaves (Gatherer) - Tying up bundles of harvested crops.
5. Threshing (Dosh) - Separating grain from the husks.
6. Winnowing (Zoreh) - Separating the chaff from the grain.
7. Selecting (Borer) - Sorting or choosing different types of materials.
8. Grinding (Tochein) - Grinding or milling.
9. Sifting (Meraked) - Sifting flour or other substances.
10. Kneading (Losh) Kneading dough or similar substances.
11. Baking (Ofeh) - Baking or cooking.
12. Shearing wool (Gozez) - Removing wool from an animal.
13. Washing wool (Melabein) - Cleaning Wool.
14. Beating wool (Menapeitz) - Beating or carding wool.
15. Dyeing (Toveh) - Colouring or dyeing materials.
16. Spinning (Meishiv) - Spinning thread or yarn.
17. Weaving (Oseh) - Weaving fabric or creating a textile.
18. Making two loops (Koshair) - Creating knots or loops.
19. Weaving two threads (Mokeh b'Patish) - Joining threads or materials.
20. Separating two threads (Tear apart) - Separating threads or materials.
21. Tying a knot (Tzad) - Tying a knot that will last.
22. Untying a knot (Matir) - Untying a permanent knot.
23. Sewing (Tofer) - Sewing or stitching materials together.
24. Tearing (Koreah) - Tearing or ripping materials.
25. Trapping (Tzad) - Trapping or catching animals.
26. Slaughtering (Shocheit) - Ritual animal slaughter.
27. Flaying (Mafshit) - Skinning an animal.
28. Salting (Me'abed) - Preserving meat through salting.
29. Curing (Melabain) - Preserving hides or materials.
30. Scraping (Memacheik) - Scraping animal hide or similar actions.
31. Cutting to shape (Soser) - Shaping materials for a specific purpose.

32. Writing (Kotev) - Writing or inscribing.
33. Erasing (Mochek) - Erasing or removing writing.
34. Building (Boneh) - Constructing or building.
35. Demolishing (Soser) - Dismantling or destroying structures.
36. Extinguishing a flame (Mechabeh) - Extinguishing a fire or flame.
37. Igniting a flame (Mav'ir) - Lighting a flame or fire.
38. Striking the final blow (Makeh b'Patish) - Completing the final step of a process.
39. Transferring between domains (Hotza'ah) - Carrying or transporting items between domains.

The 39 categories that define what work is prohibited on Shabbat in traditional Judaism mainly cover tasks related to farming and craftsmanship. These categories provide a fascinating glimpse into the past, but their direct application to modern life can sometimes be limited. Many of the prohibitions involve tasks that are rare today, like threshing and winnowing, which might be difficult for people in contemporary society to relate to or understand.

Additionally, the specific jobs mentioned within these categories don't cover the wide variety of professions and trades in the modern world. This discrepancy leads to challenges in adapting and applying these ancient rules to today's diverse job landscape, making it hard to match modern professions directly with the original 39 categories.

As a result, Jewish communities worldwide have made various efforts to bridge the gap between these traditional categories and the evolving nature of work, careers, and occupations. This has led to diverse practices and interpretations within Judaism, reflecting the ongoing effort to reconcile these ancient rules with contemporary life.

So, it's important to note that these categories' practical applications and interpretations can vary significantly among

Jewish communities and individuals. Consulting with a knowledgeable Rabbi or studying the specific guidelines of one's community is advised for a more comprehensive understanding of the restrictions and traditions.

But one thing about this day is common throughout Judaism. Shabbat, the day of rest and spiritual enrichment, celebrates God's creation of the world and serves as a time dedicated to family, community, and prayer. On Shabbat, people abstain from work to concentrate on spiritual and personal growth, fostering a deeper connection with God.

There are many Jewish traditions associated with Shabbat. Here are a few of the main ones most commonly accepted and observed.

1. Observance: Shabbat is a day of rest, modelled after the Biblical account of God resting on the seventh day of creation. Observing and keeping the Shabbat is considered a mitzvah (commandment).
2. Preparation: Before the arrival of Shabbat, Jewish households engage in preparations known as erev Shabbat. This includes cleaning the home, preparing special meals, and setting the dining table with festive items for the family meal.
3. Candle lighting tradition. Jewish women traditionally light at least two candles before Shabbat starts. This is usually done at least 18 minutes before sunset, accompanied by a specific blessing. Although the Torah does not explicitly mention candle lighting, this tradition likely developed because Jewish law prohibits kindling a fire on Shabbat. The exact reason for lighting two candles is not entirely apparent, but one common interpretation is that they symbolise the sanctity and peace of Shabbat, marking the distinction between the regular weekdays and the sacred day of rest.

4. Blessings: Before the meal begins, many sing *Shalom Aleichem*, and some families will also recite the blessing over the children at this point or sing *Eshet Chayil* (Proverbs 31:10-31). These are all customs, however, and are not mandated by Jewish law
5. Blessing over wine: A special blessing, known as Kiddush, is recited over a cup of wine or grape juice. The Hebrew word *Kiddush* means sanctification, and this ritual is to sanctify Shabbat. It signifies the transition into the sacred day. The reason for using wine or grape juice for Kiddush on Friday nights in Judaism is not universally agreed upon; it was established as law by the Talmudic Sages between 150 and 500 C.E., with some believing it's due to wine's role in gladdening man. Others link it to celebrating Shabbat as a bride, akin to wedding celebrations.
6. HaMotzi: Before the meal, after Kiddush is recited over the wine, a blessing known as HaMotzi is said over the Challah, a braided bread traditionally made with eggs, which has become synonymous with Shabbat. Two loaves are often used. This originated in the Torah because when the Israelites wandered in the desert post-Exodus, God commanded them to bring in a double portion of manna before Shabbat. These blessings express gratitude for our blessed provisions and are an essential part of the Shabbat meal.
7. Festive meals: Shabbat is traditionally celebrated with family and friends, and it is customary to have festive meals on Friday night. These meals often include special foods and dishes, such as challah, traditional Jewish recipes, and other symbolic foods.
8. Rest and prohibition of work: Shabbat is a day of rest, and observant Jews refrain from certain activities defined as work in Jewish law. This includes the prohibitions listed

under the 39 definitions given above. Many of these activities have been refined in the modern world, including using electronic devices, cooking, driving and conducting business transactions. The focus is spiritual reflection, spending time with family, and engaging in prayer and study.

9. Synagogue services: Jews often attend synagogue services on Shabbat, which can be on Friday evening, Saturday morning, or Saturday afternoon. The number of services and those attending varies across the spectrum of Jewish communities. The synagogue becomes a central hub for communal worship and study. It includes prayer, reading from the Torah, and a sermon on the weekly Torah portion, usually given by the Rabbi.
10. Family time: Shabbat allows families to come together and spend quality time together. It is a time for shared meals, conversations, singing, reading from the Torah, studying other Jewish texts, and engaging in Religious discussions. Above all, it's to be a time of gratitude and joy.
11. Havdalah: Havdalah is a brief ceremony that marks the end of Shabbat. It takes place on Saturday evening after sunset. Wine or grape juice is used, and a braided candle is lit. Prayers and blessings are recited, bidding farewell to the sanctity of Shabbat and welcoming the new week. The candle is then extinguished, signifying the separation of the Holy Shabbat day from the working week.

Shabbat holds great spiritual and cultural importance for Jews. It is considered a day of rest, reflection, and connection with family, community, and God. It provides a much-needed break from the busyness of daily life and allows individuals to recharge their spiritual Batteries.

These are just a few of the many Jewish traditions and benefits associated with Shabbat. The specific customs and practices can vary among different Jewish communities and individuals. Still, the underlying principle of setting aside this day for rest, worship, family, and community remains consistent.

Shabbat from a Messianic Jewish perspective.

As with any form of Judaism, there are significant variations in how Shabbat is viewed and celebrated within the Messianic movement. However, there is one thing that all forms of Judaism, including Messianic, agree on and have in common: Shabbat is to be observed, regardless of how we define work and what traditions and rituals we incorporate into it.

In the New Covenant, numerous passages highlight Shabbat within the context of Yeshua's teachings, ministry, and the practices of the Jewish community at that time. It's essential to recognise that Yeshua was a devout follower of the Torah, raised in a family committed to its observance. Throughout his life, he consistently upheld the Torah, including the principles of keeping Shabbat.

Contrary to contemporary misconceptions, especially within the church, Sha'ul (Paul) strived to obey the Torah. He never advocated against any of its commandments, including observing the Shabbat.

Yeshua fully expected the observance of Shabbat to persist well beyond his time on earth. In a conversation with the crowd, shortly before his death, resurrection, and ascension, regarding the future destruction of the second temple - an event he knew would occur long after his departure - he shared with them:

"Pray it doesn't happen in winter or on the Shabbat". Matthew 24:25

If Yeshua had come to do away with the keeping of the Shabbat, this is a warning that he wouldn't have given. Sha'ul, the Disciples, Apostles, and early believers would have known that and ceased to observe it. Reading through the New Covenant clarifies that they all kept the Torah, including observing and keeping the Shabbat.

Here are some key places Shabbat is mentioned in the New Covenant:

Mark 2:27-28. *"Then Yeshua said to them, 'The Shabbat was made for man, not man for the Shabbat.'"*

Matthew 12:1-14. This passage tells the story of Yeshua's disciples' plucking grain on the Shabbat. These actions sparked debates between Yeshua and the Pharisees about the spirit of Shabbat observances.

Luke 13:10-17. This passage recounts Yeshua healing a woman bent over for eighteen years on the Shabbat and His defence of performing such acts of healing on the Shabbat.

Luke 14:1-6. Another instance is Yeshua healing a man with dropsy on the Shabbat and then discussing acts of mercy and healing with Pharisees on that day.

John 5:1-18. This passage describes Yeshua healing a paralysed man at the pool of Bethesda on Shabbat. This act led to further conflicts with the religious authority about Shabbat observance.

These passages illustrate how Yeshua interacted with and interpreted the Shabbat law, often challenging the traditional understanding of it and emphasising the value of compassion and doing good, even on Shabbat.

Yeshua's perspective often differed from that of the religious leaders of his time, especially the Pharisees, who adhered strictly to the Shabbat laws. This example highlights the risk I previously discussed: traditions can sometimes overshadow the importance of God's Word if we are not careful.

Meanwhile, Yeshua emphasised the spiritual and compassionate aspects of Shabbat, concentrating his teachings on rectifying misunderstandings and underscoring the fundamental principles of its observance.

Here are some critical aspects of his teachings related to the Shabbat:

Yeshua affirmed the importance of the Shabbat as a day set apart for rest and worship. He observed Shabbat himself and always attended synagogue services.

Luke 4:16 *Now, when he went to Natzeret, where he had been brought up, on Shabbat, he went to the synagogue as usual.*

Yeshua was a vocal critic of the religious leaders of his time, particularly regarding their stringent application of rules and traditions to Shabbat. He argued that their approach missed the essence of Shabbat, emphasising instead the need for mercy and compassion even on this holy day. This perspective often put him at odds with the Pharisees, who favoured a more legalistic interpretation.

Yeshua's commitment to his beliefs was evident in his actions. He frequently performed healing miracles on Shabbat, acts that stirred controversy but powerfully demonstrated his point. These miracles were not just acts of compassion; they were also symbolic, illustrating that caring for others and addressing their needs was in keeping with the true spirit of Shabbat.

Moreover, Yeshua taught that the purpose of Shabbat was to serve humanity, not to be a source of undue burden. He highlighted the day's importance for rest, worship, and compassion, emphasising that Shabbat observance should align with these values. In doing so, he challenged the prevailing legalistic interpretations and prioritised human well-being over rigid adherence to rules.

Examining the New Covenant writings, we see how Yeshua and His disciples observed Shabbat in the same way as others in the Judaism of their time. Far from suggesting that Shabbat would be abolished or altered with His coming, Yeshua affirmed the ongoing importance of keeping this commandment.

He made it unmistakable that Shabbat would remain unchanged. Neither He nor the apostles introduced any alterations to the day, its principles, or its practices.

We can see this from further writings in the New Covenant.

Acts 13:14, 42-44. These passages mention the apostles going to the synagogue on Shabbat to preach the Gospel.

Acts:15:19-21. Here, James outlines some requirements for Gentile believers.

"So it is my judgement that we should not cause extra difficulty for those among the Gentiles who are turning to God. Instead, we should write a letter telling them to abstain from things polluted by idols, from sexual immorality, from what is strangled, and from blood. For from ancient times Moses has had those who proclaim him in every city since he is being read in the synagogues every Shabbat."

Moses being proclaimed pertains to the Torah being publicly read every Shabbat at the synagogue. The expectation was clear: Gentiles who had embraced faith in Yeshua were expected to attend the synagogue every Shabbat, just as Yeshua, His disciples, and all those devoted to God's Word did. There, they would gradually learn the entire Torah and gain insights into how to uphold its teachings.

Shabbat, a sacred day of rest, is central to traditional Judaism's religious practices. In Messianic Judaism, Shabbat retains its sanctity but also assumes additional significance due to beliefs in Yeshua as the Messiah.

This perspective is reflected in the New Covenant's Book of Hebrews, an open letter to Jewish communities in the diaspora. The text, especially in Hebrews 4:1-11, frequently mentions a 'Shabbat rest,' a concept rich in symbolic and theological meaning. The author of Hebrews uses the idea of Shabbat rest to express deep spiritual truths, focusing on the preeminence of Yeshua as the ultimate high priest, the final sacrifice for the forgiveness of sins, and the source of spiritual rest for believers.

In Hebrews, the notion of Shabbat rest goes beyond the physical observance of a day of rest. It represents a spiritual peace that believers find through their faith in Yeshua. The text draws a parallel to the Israelites who, due to disobedience and disbelief, failed to enter God's promised rest in their land (Hebrews 3:16-19). The author then connects this historical narrative to contemporary readers, urging them not to harden their hearts and miss the opportunity for eternal rest offered by God through Yeshua.

Shabbat or Lord's Day?

Having explored the traditional Jewish and Messianic views on Shabbat, including its significance, symbolism, and customary practices, we now turn our attention to an important question: How and why was the God-ordained day of rest, worship, and teaching changed for so many believers from the Biblically mandated seventh-day Shabbat to Sunday, and renamed the Lord's Day?

This transformation, which we will briefly examine here, directly contradicts and opposes God's teachings as outlined in His Word. The evolution of this practice over several decades involved numerous individuals, groups, and events, making it impossible to attribute the change to any single cause or person. A series of events gradually led to these deviations from God's Word, significantly influencing the early gentile church. Consequently, this will only be a brief and simplified overview of the early centuries when these shifts in Shabbat observance occurred.

In the Genesis creation narrative, God worked for six days and rested on the seventh, sanctifying it as Holy. Then, He commanded us to emulate this pattern, working for six days and resting on the seventh to remember His creation.

It is evident from the Messianic Writings that Yeshua, the Apostles, and the early Jewish believers adhered to the Torah, which meant continuing to observe Shabbat as God commanded.

Scripture nowhere indicates that Yeshua came to teach anyone to abandon Torah adherence, keeping God's commandments - just the opposite. The early believers were all Torah-observant Jews who continued to meet in synagogues.

Therefore, they would not have considered changing the traditional day of rest. Such a change would contradict God's commandments, which they would never contemplate.

Significantly, for nearly a decade after Yeshua's ascension, the New Covenant does not mention any Gentile believers. The centurion Cornelius is the first Gentile believer recorded in Acts chapter 10.

Peter's sermon in Acts chapter 2 was addressed solely to Jews, as evident to anyone reading the text. It tells us that many Jews from every nation had travelled to Yerushalayim for the Shavuot festival in obedience to the Torah and heard his message. From that number, over 3,000 believed and were baptised, and they were all Jews.

(Before we dive into the discussion, we must clear up a common misunderstanding. The practice of baptism, known as Mikvah in Hebrew, originated in the Hebrew Scriptures long before the Christian church embraced it.

The Mikvah plays a crucial role in Jewish religious life, serving as a symbol of spiritual rebirth. It's not just about physical cleansing; it represents a more profound spiritual purification and renewal. Immersing oneself in natural flowing waters, like the River Jordan, is laden with symbolism - it signifies life, purification, and a fresh start.

The focus on using flowing water highlights a link to the act of divine creation and marks a significant moment of personal spiritual awakening. This ritual underlines the importance placed by Judaism on not just physical cleanliness but also the purity of the spirit, emphasising a holistic approach to spiritual well-being).

Contrary to what many accept and teach, Peter's sermon and the number of those who believed did not represent the church's birth. As we have seen, these were Messianic Jews, Jews who accepted that Yeshua was the long-awaited Messiah and who, for decades afterwards, met in synagogues and homes. The word church does not appear anywhere in the original Greek text, and it was several decades before the word Christian was used.

The term "Christian" first appears in Acts 11:26, about ten years after Yeshua lived. This term emerged during the apostles' visit to Antioch, where they spread the message of salvation. Before being called "Christians," Acts 11:19 points out that the apostles initially focused their preaching on Jews rather than Gentiles.

However, soon after, the message began to reach Gentiles, leading some to embrace the Messianic faith. These new Gentile believers did not form a separate religion but instead joined the existing faith of the Messianic Jews. There is no scriptural basis to suggest that these Gentile believers established a separate faith called Christianity or created a new place of worship called church distinct from that of the Jewish believers.

The term "Christ" is the Greek translation of the Hebrew word "Mashiach" (Messiah), indicating the anointed one. Greek-speaking individuals used this term to describe both Jewish believers and the few Gentiles who had recently joined them. According to scripture, these Gentiles were "grafted into" the olive tree, which symbolised Israel, indicating their inclusion into the Messianic Jewish faith rather than creating a new separate religion.

Acts 18:1-2 tells of Aquila and Priscilla, Messianic Jewish believers in Yeshua, who were expelled from Rome, not for their Christian faith but for being Jews.

After this, Sha'ul left Athens and went to Corinth, where he met a Jewish man named Aquila, originally from Pontus but having recently come with his wife Priscilla from Italy because Claudius had issued a decree expelling all the Jews from Rome.

Even two decades after Yeshua, Acts 21:20 reveals that thousands of Jewish believers remained committed to the Torah, including honouring Shabbat as the day of rest.

When they heard this, they praised God. Then they said to Paul:

*"You see, brother, how many **thousands** of Jews have believed, and **all of them** are zealous for the law"*.

These Messianic Jews, zealous for the law, diligently adhered to God's commands in the Torah, including keeping the Shabbat on the seventh day. This practice, supported by biblical and historical evidence, continued well into the first century.

However, a significant shift occurred over time, with some believers beginning to observe their rest day on Sunday instead of the traditional Saturday Shabbat, contrary to the commandment in the Bible. This change, which deviates from the practices of Yeshua, his disciples, and early followers, has led to considerable debate among biblical scholars, as the Bible does not endorse this transition.

Understanding this shift requires careful examination of Scripture, its language, and historical context. Both Messianic Jews and Gentile believers initially observed the Sabbath as instructed, raising questions about the reasons and authority behind changing the worship day to Sunday, a move contradicting biblical teachings, Yeshua's instructions, and the practices of his early followers.

Many attribute this change to celebrating the Messiah's resurrection on a Sunday, the first day of the week, often called The Lord's Day. This change and other early changes in the faith marked the beginning of the new Gentile Christian faith's divergence from its purely Jewish roots, often replacing original Biblical instructions with human interpretations not found anywhere in Scripture.

The word 'church' exemplifies such alterations. The Greek word 'ekklesia' describes any gathering or assembly, including those for political or religious discussions.

'Ekklesia', as used in the New Testament, simply referred to a meeting of Jewish followers and the Gentiles who had joined them. Later translations changed it to 'church' to give the impression of a separate gathering and intentionally distancing the new Christian faith from its Messianic Jewish origins. This shift led to several errors in the church, including misrepresenting Yeshua's true nature as a Jew who followed and taught adherence to the Torah.

The change in the day of worship from Saturday to Sunday is often attributed to a passage in the Book of Revelation, specifically chapter 1, verse 10, where John states,

"I was in the spirit on the Lord's day, and I heard behind me a loud voice like a trumpet saying, 'Write in a book what you see.'"

As further explored later in this book, the Torah designates a specific day for remembering Yeshua's resurrection, an annual event not referred to as the 'The Lord's Day' or easter.

Bible translations vary in wording, mainly due to the challenges of directly translating some phrases. As a result, the term 'The Lord's Day' appears with varying frequency across different Bible versions, from as little as once to as many as 23 times.

This phrase is often associated with references in Scriptures like 2 Peter 3:10, 2 Thessalonians 2:2, and Malachi 4:5, which signify God's judgement day, or 'the Day of the Lord.'

However, the specific Greek term for 'The Lord's Day' (ἡ κυριακὴ ἡμέρα) is only found once in the entire Greek Bible, on this one occasion in Revelation, and a thorough examination of the Scriptures, especially in the original Greek, reveals no verse directly, or even indirectly, connecting 'The Lord's Day' to the Messiah's resurrection.

This raises the question: what does this term signify? The term 'The Lord's Day' appears only in Revelation, while the similar term, 'the Day of the Lord,' is frequently used throughout Scripture to refer to God's future intervention and judgement.

The 'Day of the Lord' is often depicted as a time of wrath and judgement, as described by prophets like Isaiah, Joel, Amos, and Zephaniah. This concept is closely linked to the end times and the final judgement, as discussed by Sha'ul in his letters, where it is associated with the return of Yeshua and the establishment of God's Kingdom.

The content of Revelation strongly suggests that John's vision is more likely related to the 'Day of the Lord', God's future judgement, rather than an instruction to alter the day of worship. This interpretation aligns far better with the broader scriptural context.

Nevertheless, while the exact meaning of 'The Lord's Day', as mentioned by John, remains uncertain, it seems more plausible to associate it with future events rather than an alteration to God's command concerning Shabbat observance.

Furthermore, references to the first day of the week in the New Covenant do not suggest a celebration or worship day for the Lord's resurrection, nor do they imply it should replace the Shabbat.

The early believers' practice of breaking bread on the first day of the week, mentioned in Scripture, was simply a communal meal, not a redefinition of the day's significance.

Long after the apostles' deaths, the transition from the God-ordained Shabbat to Sunday worship evolved from theological, historical, and cultural factors. This change was a human decision, not a divine directive.

As the number of Gentile converts increased, many doctrines gradually evolved and changed, making it challenging to trace the timeline and understand the specific changes precisely.

In Rome, the centre of the Roman Empire, the influx of Gentile believers increased Roman influence. This shift became more pronounced after the destruction of the Second Temple in CE70, and following the Bar Kochba-led revolt in CE132-136, which led to the Jewish exile. Consequently, the Jewish leadership of the believers relocated from Yerushalayim to Rome.

As we have seen, many thousands of early followers were initially Messianic Jews. Soon, the growing number of Gentile converts began to outnumber the Jewish believers, steering the faith towards a predominantly Gentile composition and, subsequently, Gentile leadership. During this period, Rome was a melting pot of various religious groups, including Pagans, Messianic Jews, Gentile Christians, and traditional Jews, each vying for dominance.

This competition led to significant doctrinal changes and compromises as efforts were made to reconcile these diverse beliefs. Over time, these concessions gradually altered the original teachings of Yeshua and the Apostles, which were rooted in Messianic Judaism. Sometimes, these changes were made for integration and others for acceptance within the broader religious landscape.

One notable change aimed at unifying these diverse religions was the shift of the worship day from the Shabbat to Sunday, aligning with the day when the majority, predominantly Pagans, worshipped their sun god, Sol Invictus.

Similarly, December 25th, the festival of Sol Invictus, was adopted as the date for celebrating the birth of the Messiah. This adaptation reflected the prevailing cultural and religious influences of the time.

In religious art, especially in church stained glass windows, you may notice a bright yellow circle around the heads of early believers, even those of Yeshua and his mother. This circle represents the sun god, not a divine halo. This image shows how Christianity, whose name comes from the Greek word for 'Messianic,' mixed with pagan sun worship practices. This blending of beliefs significantly impacted Church teachings and faith to the point where some of it could even be considered idolatry.

It's important to understand that "sun worship" in this context refers to the veneration of the sun and various solar deities across different ancient civilisations. Many cultures incorporated sun worship into their religious practices, viewing the sun as a symbol of life, light, and fertility. Deities like Ra in Egypt and Sol Invictus in Rome were central to these traditions.

The Romans, in particular, were well known for adopting and assimilating many aspects of other cultures into their religious practices. They also often blended in various festivals of their and others' faiths.

Making converts to what had originally been known as Messianic Judaism but was now rapidly being termed the Christian faith because of the language used, and the growing persecution of all forms of Judaism also provided many challenges for evangelism.

The problem for most people was their being asked to turn their backs on having other gods, not only because of how they had been raised but also because of the potential penalty that could be incurred for doing so. To ease this transition and make Christianity more palatable, some began adapting pagan festivals and practices into their new form of Christianity to make it more acceptable and more appealing to the people.

For example, the celebration of the birth of the Messiah on December 25th, calling it Christmas, the birth of Christ, was strategically placed near the time of the winter solstice, an essential solar celebration in many cultures. This blending was simply done to be more attractive to potential followers and cause less conflict with those around them. It was making it what we call today 'seeker-friendly' at the expense of the truth.

Over time, all the believers became known by the Greek term Christian, and gradually, the move away from Judaic practices became more and more pronounced. Finally, anything deemed even slightly Jewish, which threatened to challenge these changes, became banned, and anyone seen as being Torah-obedient was severely persecuted, even put to death.

This included the commandment of observing the seventh day Shabbat and the obligation to celebrate the festivals as ordained by God in Scripture. Sunday, reserved initially for sun worship, became the convenient substitute for Shabbat and soon gained widespread acceptance.

Additionally, new celebrations were introduced to replace the festivals that were deemed "too Jewish". But these God-given festivals had deep significance, including commemorating Yeshua's birth, death, and resurrection and those pointing to future Messianic events. So much was lost when they were ignored, and those who openly resisted these alterations and sought to remain faithful to Scripture faced severe consequences.

The council of Laodicea in CE363 played a significant role in formalising this transition from Shabbat observation to recognising Sunday as the day of worship for Christians and discouraging the Jewish Shabbat observance, along with what was now seen as the 'Jewish festivals' rather than as 'God's appointed times'. So, some Moedim were replaced with man-devised, easily acceptable alternatives or banned altogether.

The whole melting pot of beliefs was ultimately ruled over by the leader of the Roman Empire, who had the final say in what happened. This cultural syncretism was seen as the best way of bringing and keeping some kind of unity in his empire. As the gentile leadership of the newly forming Christian faith was based in Rome, it became known as the church of Rome. The word catholic simply means universal, so it took on the title of the Roman Catholic church, often putting the word holy in front of it to give it the appearance of being of God. Because the Roman Empire covered such a vast area, it took time for these proclamations to spread. Hence, this formalisation took time to filter through to the entire empire.

And a closer study of the Scriptures reveals that all this was done without any Biblical basis. It went totally against much of the Word of God. The Word of God was negated for man's traditions. It is just as Yeshua said in Mark 7:8-9;

"You disobey God's commands in order to obey what humans have taught. You are good at rejecting God's commands so that you can follow your own teachings!"

The following are just a few quotes from the church, confessing how it was the church that changed the Shabbat from Saturday to Sunday and even admitting to its lack of Biblical foundation for doing so. Consider them carefully and compare them with what Scripture tells us.

Bishop Thomas Enright stated, *"There is but one church on the face of the earth - the catholic church - that has the power to make laws binding on the conscience, binding before God, binding under the pain of hellfire. You say it is to obey the commandment, 'Remember the Shabbat day to keep it Holy.' But Sunday is not the Shabbat according to the Bible and the record of time. Everyone knows that Sunday is the first day of the week, while Saturday is the seventh day and the Shabbat, the day consecrated as a day of rest. It was the holy catholic church that changed the day of rest from Saturday to Sunday"*. (Father Enright on the Sunday, printed in the American Sentinel).

"Is Saturday the seventh day according to the Bible and the ten commandments? I answer, yes. Is Sunday the first day of the week and did the church change the seventh - Saturday - for Sunday, the first day? I answer, yes. Did Christ change the day? I answer, no. You may read the Bible from Genesis to Revelation, and you will not find a single line authorising the sanctification of Sunday". (James Cardinal Gibbons, Archbishop of Baltimore).

"It is now commonly held that God simply gave His church the power to set aside whatever day or days she would deem suitable as Holy days. The church chose Sunday, the first day of the week, and in the course of time added other days as holy days". (Rev John Laux, A course in Religion for Catholic high schools and academies).

"Practically everything that protestants regard as essential or important they have received from the Catholic church. They accepted Sunday rather than Saturday as the day for public worship after the Catholic Church made that change. But the protestant mind does not seem to realise that in accepting the Bible, in observing the Sunday, in keeping Christmas and Easter, they are accepting the authority of the spokesman for the church, the pope". (Our Sunday visitor, February 5th, 1950.

"The Roman church appeal as well to the transference of the Shabbat to Sunday - contrary to the ten commandments. No other example is so strongly emphasised and quoted as the transference of the Shabbat. Thereby they want to maintain that the power of the church is great, because it has dispensed with and altered part of the ten commandments". (Philip Melanchthon, The Augsburg Confession).

"The festival of Sunday, like all other festivals, was always only a human ordinance, and it was far from the intentions of the apostles to establish a divine command in this respect, far from them, and from the early apostolic church, to transfer the laws of the Shabbat

Chapter 6.

Rosh Chodesh

We started our trip through God's appointed times by considering the most repeated event, the weekly Shabbat. Before we go onto the seasonal Moedim, let's briefly look at the second most frequently commemorated celebration, Rosh Chodesh.

Rosh Chodesh, meaning "head of the month" in Hebrew, is the Jewish holiday that marks the beginning of a new lunar month in the Hebrew calendar. The Hebrew calendar is lunisolar, which means it is based on the moon's cycles, but it also incorporates adjustments to keep it synchronised with the solar year.

In the Hebrew calendar, months vary between 29 and 30 days, depending on the lunar cycle. Rosh Chodesh occurs on the first day of each new lunar month when the moon's first crescent becomes visible after the dark moon.

The observance of Rosh Chodesh is mentioned in several places in the Hebrew Scriptures (the Old Testament):

1. Numbers 10:10: *"Also in the day of your gladness, and in your appointed feasts, and in the beginnings of your months, you shall blow with the shofar over your burnt offerings, and over the sacrifices of your peace offerings; that they may be to you for a memorial before your God: I am the LORD your God."*

2. 1 Samuel 20:5: *"And David said to Jonathan, Behold, tomorrow is the new moon, and I should sit with the king at meat: but let me go, that I may hide myself in the field unto the third day at even."*

3. 2 Kings 4:23: *He asked, "Why are you going to him today? It isn't Rosh-Chodesh, and it isn't Shabbat."*

4. Psalms 81:3: *"Blow upon the Shofar in the new moon, in the time appointed, on our solemn feast day."*

5. Isaiah 66:23: *"And it shall come to pass, that from one new moon to another, and from one Shabbat to another, shall all flesh come to worship before me, saith the LORD."*

In these verses, Rosh Chodesh is associated with blowing Shofars, appointed feasts, gladness, and solemn worship. The Jewish people traditionally observe Rosh Chodesh as a minor holiday with special prayers, readings, and gatherings.

The celebration of Rosh Chodesh has commonly been considered a special day for Jewish women, but, like all festivals, the celebration of Rosh Chodesh varies among different Jewish communities. Some standard practices include:

1. Special blessings are recited to mark the occasion. These blessings often thank God for bringing the new month and ask for a month filled with goodness and blessings.

2. Specific prayers and readings associated with Rosh Chodesh are added to the regular synagogue services. These prayers often focus on themes of renewal and the significance of the new month.

3. Some families or communities are accustomed to enjoying a festive meal to celebrate Rosh Chodesh. It can include traditional Jewish dishes and provides an additional opportunity for families and friends to come together.

4. As mentioned earlier, Rosh Chodesh has often been considered a special day for Jewish women. In some communities, women may have gatherings or study sessions on this day, emphasising its significance to women's spirituality and communal role.

5. In many synagogues, the Psalms of Hallel (Psalms 113-118) are recited or sung during morning prayers on Rosh Chodesh, similar to their use on other holidays.

6. Unlike major Jewish holidays, Rosh Chodesh is not a Shabbat day of rest, and there are generally no restrictions on work or other activities.

It's essential to note that practices vary among Jewish communities and denominations, and some may observe Rosh Chodesh more prominently. In contrast, others may have fewer, if any, associated customs. It is worth noting that the Scripture gives us very few instructions on how to keep it. One of the few is that we are to hear the sound of the shofar, the trumpet.

Remember that while the concept of Rosh Chodesh is found in the Scriptures, many specific customs and practices related to its observance, as with those of all the Moedim, feasts, fasts, and festivals, have been developed over time in rabbinic Judaism based on later interpretations and traditions.

Overall, Rosh Chodesh is considered a time of renewal and reflection, ushering in the blessings of a new month in the Jewish calendar.

Rosh Chodesh from a Messianic Jewish perspective.

In Traditional Judaism, Rosh Chodesh is a minor holiday often marked with special prayers and blessings. Some Messianic Jews interpret Rosh Chodesh in light of their belief in Yeshua as the Messiah and see symbolic connections to His role in fulfilling prophecies and establishing the Messianic age.

While there is no unified Messianic view of Rosh Chodesh, some possible interpretations could include believers seeing Rosh Chodesh as a time of renewal and hope for the future, anticipating the ultimate redemption and restoration promised by the Messiah.

Also, since the new moon represents a tiny sliver of light emerging from darkness, some Messianic believers might associate this with Yeshua, the light of the world who brings illumination and salvation.

While some Messianic Jews emphasise Rosh Chodesh and incorporate elements into their celebration and worship, others might not observe it in any distinct way. As with all religious perspectives, interpretations can vary among individuals and communities within the Messianic Jewish movement.

Chapter 7.

Pesach - Can we just Passover it?

"In every generation, one is obliged to regard himself as if he personally had come out of Egypt." Pesachim 116b

Many people know the famous musical "Joseph and the Amazing Technicolor Dreamcoat" by Andrew Lloyd Webber and Tim Rice. It's based on the Biblical story of Joseph from Genesis, but it's certainly not a strict adaptation. The musical adds its own flair and doesn't precisely follow the Pesach story in the Bible. It's more about entertainment than an accurate retelling of the Biblical events.

But, it's common for people to learn history from movies or musicals rather than studying the actual events. However, for those raised in practising Jewish homes, understanding and observing Jewish traditions, including the Moedim (appointed times), is a natural part of life.

There's a lot to learn for newcomers to Judaism, particularly those from a Church background exploring Messianic Judaism. The Church often omits the Moedim commanded in Scripture, leading many to misunderstand their significance. Unfortunately, this means many are missing out on the depth of God's messages in these events, including insights into His plans for redemption and salvation.

The Moedim are seasonal events commanded in Scripture. Besides Shabbat and Rosh Chodesh, there are seven, split between spring and autumn, with one between those groups. By observing these events, we can better understand God's plan for humanity. As we conclude this first book covering these events, we will gain a clearer view of God's overall plan and its specific timeline.

The first moed is the spring feast called Pesach, more often known as Passover. This is one of the most widely celebrated Jewish holidays, commemorating and marking the liberation of the Israelites from slavery in ancient Egypt.

The Pesach story, starting in the Book of Genesis and continuing into the Book of Exodus, recounts the events of the Israelites' enslavement in Egypt, Moses' leadership, the Ten Plagues, and the eventual liberation and redemption of the Israelites, God's chosen people, from slavery.

For anyone studying God's Moedim, it is essential to begin the journey through the Moedim here, not because it comes first in our Gregorian calendar or the Biblical Jewish New Year, but because it represents redemption, and that has to be the starting point in our journey.

Everything begins with redemption. Without it, our faith journey goes nowhere. Redemption is at the heart of Pesach, is at the heart of our faith and is the beginning of God's plan of salvation for us.

The Pesach festival is a significant and bustling time, celebrated over seven or eight days depending on the Jewish tradition and geographic location. This period encompasses two other important events: haMatzot (Unleavened Bread) and haBikkurim (First Fruits), which we will explore in the following two chapters. These events are often included as part of the Pesach week because they closely relate to it and occur near this festival.

It's crucial to recognise that Pesach, haMatzot, and haBikkurim are not a single festival, even though they may seem to be celebrated together. Each has its unique significance in the Jewish calendar. They play distinct yet interconnected roles in illustrating God's plan and timeline for redemption. Overlooking their importance and treating the entire Pesach period as one single event risks missing vital messages about God's intentions.

Pesach begins on the 14th day of the Hebrew month of Nisan and is followed on the 15th day by HaMatzah. The HaBikkurim festival falls the day after the first day of HaMatzah, the 16th of Nisan. As I've just stated, each of these three festivals, while often regarded and celebrated as one, will be explained separately here because, as you will learn, they all have massive Messianic implications.

But let's deal with Pesach first. It's the story of how, first through the life of Joseph and then of Moses, God saved his chosen people, initially from a great famine that swept through the land and then from the horrors of slavery in Egypt.

Scripture contains several references to Pesach, particularly in the Old Covenant. Here are some key passages.

1. Exodus 12:1-14: This section describes the institution of the Pesach observance. It outlines the instructions God gave Moses and Aaron regarding preparing and consuming the Pesach meal and the significance of the lamb's blood on the doorposts as a sign for the Israelites to be saved from the final plague.

2. Exodus 12:15-20: These verses provide guidelines for the observance of the feast of unleavened bread, which is closely linked to Pesach. The Israelites were instructed to remove all leavened bread from their houses for a week and eat only unleavened bread.

3. Exodus 12:21-28: This passage describes the actual event of the first Pesach. The Israelites followed God's instructions, sacrificed the Pesach lamb, and marked their doorposts with its blood. As a result, the Lord passed over their houses, sparing the firstborn, while the Egyptians' firstborns were struck down.

4. Exodus 13:3-10: These verses emphasise the importance of remembering and retelling the story of the Exodus from Egypt to future generations during the Pesach feast. God commanded the Israelites to observe this commemoration annually as a perpetual ordinance.

5. Leviticus 23:4-8: This chapter outlines the appointed feasts of the Lord, including Pesach. It provides specific instructions on the timing, duration, and offerings associated with the Pesach and the feast of unleavened bread.

All these passages offer a glimpse into the Biblical accounts of the origin and observances of Pesach. It is important to note that Jewish tradition and interpretations, as found in the Talmud and other rabbinic writings, further expand upon the practices and rituals often associated with Pesach. Although these writings are not Scriptural in origin, they can often help our understanding of the way the event is celebrated.

Before the start of the Pesach week, Jews thoroughly cleanse their homes, synagogues, and sometimes even their cars to remove all traces of chametz (leavened products or yeast). This removal of the slightest trace of yeast-related products, including bread, pasta, cakes, and many other similar products, serves as a reminder of the speed at which the Israelites had to leave their homes to flee the slavery in Egypt, as they didn't even have time to allow their bread to rise.

For the eight days of Pesach, consumption and possession of these goods is prohibited. An unleavened bread called matzah is eaten during this period. However, there can be slight variations among different Jewish communities, with other foods, such as legumes, also sometimes removed for this festival's duration.

Pesach is a time for Jewish people to gather with family and friends, retell the story of their ancestor's liberation, express gratitude, and reflect on the themes of freedom and redemption.

This main gathering is done at the Pesach Seder meal, held on Pesach's first night. This meal is a crucial aspect of the festival. It is accompanied by a structured ritual that involves retelling the Exodus story, consuming symbolic foods, and reciting prayers and blessings. The Haggahah, a particular text, guides the Seder and provides the order of the rituals.

Haggadah comes from the Hebrew root 'hgd,' which means 'to tell.' Thus, the Haggadah's primary purpose is to help retell the Exodus story and transmit its significance and lessons from one generation to the next. It combines prayers, blessings, songs, and explanations, making it a multi-layered narrative that engages participants in retelling the Pesach story.

While there are various versions and interpretations of the Haggadah, they generally follow a similar structure and include the following key elements:

The Seder begins with blessings over wine and washing hands.

The leader in a community, usually the Rabbi, or in a home, the head of the household welcomes the participants and sets the tone for the evening.

The retelling of the story of the Exodus is the core of the Haggadah, beginning with the hardships of Jewish slavery in Egypt, the rise of Moses as a leader, the ten plagues, and the miraculous redemption at the parting of the Red (sometimes called the Reed) Sea.

The youngest person present, who is old enough to take an active part, traditionally asks four questions that prompt the explanation of the unique customs and foods of the Seder, such as the eating of matzah and the consumption of bitter herbs.

During the Seder, participants drink four cups of wine (usually small cups for obvious reasons). The four cups of wine hold significant symbolic meaning, each representing different themes or aspects of the Pesach story, the Jewish people's relationship with God, and God's promises being fulfilled.

1. Sanctification: The first cup is known as the Cup of Sanctification. It is linked with the phrase "I will bring out" (Exodus 6:6), referring to God's promise to bring the Israelites out of Egypt. This cup is part of the Kiddush, which sanctifies the holiday.

2. Deliverance: The second cup is the Cup of Deliverance (Exodus 6:6), corresponding to the promise "I will deliver you" from slavery. This cup is drunk after reciting the story of the Exodus during the Maggid portion of the Seder.

3. Redemption: The third cup, known as the Cup of Redemption (Exodus 6:6) aligns with God's promise: "I will redeem you." It is consumed after the Birkat Hamazon, the blessing after the meal, and symbolises God's redeeming of the Israelites with an outstretched arm.

4. Acceptance: The fourth and final cup is the Cup of Acceptance or Praise, associated with God's promise, "I will take you as my people." (Exodus 6:7). This cup is drunk after the Hallel, a series of Psalms praising God, and signifies the Israelites' new relationship with God as a free people.

The Haggadah presents four archetypal sons, each with unique characteristics, representing different attitudes towards tradition and the Pesach story. This section emphasises the importance of engaging all community members, regardless of their level of knowledge or commitment.

A recitation of each of the ten plagues that afflicted Egypt as a consequence of Pharaoh's refusal to release the Israelites is done, with a drop of wine removed from the cup with a finger and dripping into the edge of a plate for each plague to acknowledge the suffering of the Egyptians. For some Jewish communities, it is also traditional to abstain from eating for the day leading up to the Pesach meal in sombre remembrance and commemoration of all the Egyptian firstborns who died.

The significance of the matzah, the unleavened bread, is explained, symbolising the haste with which the Israelites left Egypt and emphasising humility and freedom from ego.

A piece of matzah called the Afikoman is hidden during the Seder, and children search for it after the meal. The leader then shares it with all participants, symbolising the Paschal (Pesach) sacrifice and unity.

The Afikoman is a tradition rich in symbolic meaning within Jewish culture. This practice of hiding and later finding or redeeming the Afikoman is a ritual that embodies several profound themes.

One of the primary symbols associated with the Afikoman is that of hope and redemption. The act of hiding and subsequently finding the Afikoman mirrors the enduring hope and anticipated redemption of the Jewish people. This ritual serves as a poignant reminder of the Jewish journey and their unwavering faith in future salvation.

Additionally, the Afikoman signifies the continuity and resilience of Jewish tradition. By engaging in this practice, Jewish communities underscore the unbroken chain of their faith, passed down through generations. This ritual highlights the importance of preserving traditions and maintaining a strong connection to one's cultural and religious heritage.

Furthermore, the search for the Afikoman is instrumental in involving younger community members in the Seder. This aspect of the ritual is not just about participation; it symbolises the vital role of teaching and engaging the next generation. It is a metaphor for sustaining faith and the collective anticipation of the Messiah.

Another profound aspect of the Afikoman is its representation of fragmentation and eventual unification. The breaking and later reassembling of the Afikoman can be seen as a metaphor for the historical experiences of the Jewish people, particularly their dispersion and hopes for future reunification. This theme is closely intertwined with Messianic aspirations, reflecting a deeper longing for wholeness and peace.

The search for the Afikoman also provides a moment for personal and communal introspection. It allows individuals and communities to reflect on themes like freedom, redemption, and hope for a Messianic age. This reflective aspect of the ritual adds a layer of personal and communal meaning to the Seder.

It is important to note that interpretations of the Afikoman's symbolism can vary widely among Jewish communities and individuals. The message of Messianic hope and Jewish people's the symbolic significance of the Afikoman are deeply embedded in Jewish faith and tradition. Yet, they are open to personal and cultural interpretation. This flexibility in understanding underscores the richness and depth of Jewish people's ritual practice and its ability to resonate uniquely with each participant.

Birkat HaMazon, the blessing after the meal, is recited, expressing gratitude for the food and the redemption from slavery. The Seder concludes with songs of praise and hope, representing the Jewish people's faith in future redemption and a better world.

An essential element of the Pesach celebration is the Seder plate, placed centrally on the table. This is a special dish that holds specific symbolic foods that represent different aspects of the

Pesach story. Each item on the plate has significance and is an essential part of the ceremony. The arrangement and content may vary slightly depending on the cultural and regional traditions. Still, six main items are commonly found:

1. Maror (Bitter herbs): This typically consists of horseradish or another bitter vegetable. It symbolises the bitterness of slavery that the Hebrews endured in Egypt.

2. Charoset: Charoset is a mixture of chopped apples, nuts, wine or grape juice, and various spices. It represents the mortar the Hebrew enslaved people used to make the bricks for the Egyptian buildings.

3. Karpas: Karpas is a green vegetable, often parsley, dipped in salt water during the seder. The karpas represent the coming of spring and new growth, symbolising hope and renewal. It also serves as a reminder of the Jewish people's slavery in Egypt and the bitterness of that experience. The karpas are dipped into salt water during the Seder, representing the tears shed during slavery.

4. Zeroa: A roasted lamb shank bone represents the Pesach sacrifice. It serves as a reminder of God's protection during the Exodus.

5. Beitzah (hard-boiled egg): This holds symbolic significance and represents several different aspects of the Passover story:

    - Mourning and Destruction: The egg is often seen as a symbol of mourning, as it represents the destruction of the Second Temple in Yerushalayim, which was a significant event in Jewish history. The Temple's destruction is commemorated during the Pesach holiday, and the egg serves as a reminder of this tragedy.

- Circle of Life and Renewal: The egg is also associated with the cycle of life and renewal. Its round shape symbolises the cyclical nature of life and the changing seasons. Passover, occurring in the spring, is a time of rebirth and renewal; the egg reflects this theme.

- Offering: In some Jewish communities, the egg on the Seder plate represents the festival offering that used to be brought to the Temple in ancient times during Passover.

The Pesach Haggadah can vary in length, style, and additional commentaries or customs, depending on the Jewish tradition and family customs. Still, the core elements and themes remain consistent in celebrating freedom, faith, and hope.

Pesach from a Messianic Jewish perspective.

The Messianic view of Pesach is a unique perspective held by followers of Messianic Judaism and some Christian groups that combine the elements of traditional Jewish observance and the belief in Yeshua as the Messiah.

Messianic Jews typically observe the traditional customs and rituals of the Pesach seder, such as retelling the Exodus story, partaking in the symbolic foods (e.g., matzah, bitter herbs, wine), and reciting the Haggadah. During the Pesach seder, Messianic Jews also incorporate additional elements reflecting their belief in Yeshua as the Messiah.

The Afikoman, an essential part of the Passover Seder in Jewish tradition, holds special meaning in Messianic Judaism. This branch of Judaism combines traditional Jewish beliefs with the belief that Yeshua is the Messiah. For them, the Afikoman is not just a piece of matzah, or unleavened bread, but a symbol with deep Messianic significance.

During the Seder, the Afikoman is broken and hidden, later to be found by children. Messianic Jews see this as a metaphor for Yeshua's death and resurrection. The breaking of the bread represents his death, and finding the Afikoman symbolises his resurrection, which is central to their faith.

The fact that the Afikoman is unleavened is also meaningful. In scripture, yeast often represents corruption or sin, so the unleavened Afikoman reinforces the idea of Yeshua as a pure, sinless sacrifice. This ties in with the belief that Yeshua is the Passover lamb, sacrificed for humanity's sins.

Sharing the Afikoman at the Seder is also significant in Messianic Judaism. It's about remembering the Exodus and celebrating spiritual salvation through Yeshua. They believe that the benefits of Yeshua's sacrifice are shared among those who accept him, just as the Afikoman is shared among those at the Seder.

In summary, for Messianic Jews, the Afikoman is more than just a ritual item. It's a powerful symbol that links the Jewish Passover story with their beliefs about Yeshua's sacrifice and resurrection. It shows how they blend Jewish traditions with their Messianic faith, giving a unique perspective on this ancient ritual.

In addition to celebrating the historical significance of the Exodus, Messianic Jews also see Pesach as a prophecy of the ultimate redemption brought by Yeshua. Yeshua's sacrificial death is believed to represent Him as the true Pesach lamb.

Freedom from slavery in Egypt is likened in Scripture to Freedom from slavery to sin. Just as the Pesach lamb's blood was spread on the wooden doorposts to save the Israelites from slavery in Egypt, Yeshua is considered the Lamb of God, whose blood was shed on the wood of the cross to rescue His people from slavery to sin. His sacrifice brings spiritual liberation and eternal redemption.

We know from scripture that it was at the Pesach meal, which Yeshua and his disciples were observing in obedience to the Torah commandments, that Yeshua was arrested. He was then tried and executed.

A significant fact should be noted and remembered: it was on the day that Judaism commemorated the freedom from slavery to Egypt that the prophetic nature of Pesach was fulfilled. It was the day that saw the sacrificial death of Yeshua, the Pesach lamb of God, take place to save believers from their slavery to sin.

It was reported in the Gospel of John, *"Behold, the lamb of God, who takes away the sin of the world"* (John 1:29).

As we saw with the keeping of the Shabbat, not only does the festival commemorate a past event, but it also prophecies, or foreshadows a future one.

As we have seen, on Shabbat, we remember that God ceased all His work, rested on the seventh day and commanded us to stop and rest on the same day, the seventh. It pointed to when we would know the eternal Shabbat rest promised to all believers.

Now we see that it is on the very day we are commanded to keep Pesach, commemorating freedom from slavery in Egypt, that Yeshua died, providing our freedom from slavery to sin.

As the Talmud states, *"In the month of Nisan, our forefathers were redeemed from Egypt, and in the month of Nisan, we will be redeemed."* Talmud, Rosh HaShanah 11a

"In every generation, a person must see themselves as if they personally had come out of Egypt." From the Pesach Haggadah.

This emphasises the importance of reliving the Exodus story, recognising the ongoing relevance of liberation and freedom in every generation.

Chapter 8.

HaMatzot - What? No beer?

In 1957, a man called Slim Dusty had somewhat of a novelty hit record, part of whose lyrics went, "But there's nothing so lonesome, morbid or drear, than to stand in the bar of a pub with no beer."

While for those not Torah observant, it may not be a concern, for beer lovers who follow the commandments for this festival, it may come as a relief that this restriction on having a beer is only temporary because beer and all other alcoholic beverages for that matter are not allowed during the entirety of the Pesach week.

On the other hand, there could be much cheering because having to remove beer also means that Marmite is off the menu. Like all products containing even the smallest amount of yeast, they must all be removed entirely from our lives for the week. That doesn't mean only bread but all products containing any amount of yeast, no matter how small.

As we saw in the previous chapter, we are told to remove all signs of leavened products before Pesach begins, and that can create a lot of work, searching through the range of kitchen cupboards where some of these products may have been lurking unnoticed and unused for some time, to ensure that all traces are removed. This often involves emptying and washing each cupboard. It's an ideal time for an intense spring clean.

For some, eliminating these items requires sacrifice, sometimes leading to a battle of wills. Often, there is a frantic effort to remove all traces by simply eating or drinking these items before Pesach starts. However, it's best to start this process early as there is only so much beer (or Marmite) you can consume if you leave it too late.

The feast of unleavened bread, Chag HaMatzot, starts at the beginning of Pesach and continues until the end of Pesach week. Because of its proximity to the start of the week and the command to clear out all traces of yeast before Pesach starts, it's often forgotten that this is a separate God-ordained festival. It commonly becomes part of Pesach itself. But Scripture clarifies that it is a Moed in its own right.

"These are the appointed feasts of the LORD, the holy convocations, which you shall proclaim at the time appointed for them. In the first month, on the fourteenth day of the month at twilight, is the LORD's Passover. And on the fifteenth day of the same month is the Feast of Unleavened Bread to the LORD; for seven days you shall eat unleavened bread. On the first day, you shall have a holy convocation; you shall not do any ordinary work. But you shall present a food offering to the LORD for seven days. On the seventh day is a holy convocation; you shall not do any ordinary work."
Leviticus 23:4-8

There are three of the Moedim, which are pilgrimage festivals. That means that they required a man to travel to celebrate them in Yerushalayim, and this is one of them. Naturally, that would be impossible today with the millions of Jewish people scattered around the world and with the cost and time involved.

However, we know from the New Covenant writings and historical accounts that many in Biblical times did make this trip, including Yeshua and his disciples. Because it falls so close to Pesach, many travelled to Yerushalayim a day before this moed so that the priest could offer their Pesach lamb sacrifice in the temple. They could then eat the Pesach meal together in Yerushalayim.

As we previously saw, this symbolic act of removing all traces of leaven, or yeast, represents the haste in which the Hebrews left their position as enslaved people in Egypt. Chag HaMatzot holds great religious and cultural significance for Jewish people. It's a part of the time of reflection, gratitude, and remembrance of their ancestors' liberty from slavery.

HaMatzah from a Messianic Jewish perspective.

We are told in the Gospels that Yeshua and his disciples travelled to Yerushalayim to celebrate Pesach. However, for the feast of HaMatzah, which was following the commandment to be in the city for this festival, they and thousands of other Jews made this pilgrimage. As was customary, they arrived early to eat the Pesach meal in Yerushalayim. This meal that Yeshua shared with his disciples has become known as the Last Supper.

Like others of God's appointed times, Chag HaMatzot must also be viewed through a Messianic lens. In Jewish tradition and the New Covenant's writings, yeast is seen as a symbol of sin. This festival removes it from our homes and lives to signify spiritual cleansing and rededication to God.

In the Messianic view, the Feast of Unleavened Bread is a prophetic picture of Yeshua, the promised Messiah. So, while commemorating the freedom from slavery in Egypt, Messianic Jews also see this as fulfilling the prophecy that, through the Messiah's death and burial, we would be freed from slavery to sin.

When Yeshua was crucified on Pesach as the sinless Saviour, he took upon himself our sin. On Chag HaMatzot, he was buried and took our sin to the grave, where it was defeated. We shall see in the next festival how our long-prophesied salvation through the atoning work of Yeshua was completed and how this all fits in with God's plan of redemption for mankind.

Chapter 9.

HaBikkurim - First Fruits

Not a chocolate bunny or a painted egg in sight.

"The best of the first fruits of your ground you shall bring into the house of the Lord your God." Exodus 23:19

Although the festival of Bikkurim, or first fruits, is the third and final one of the spring festivals, it is, as already mentioned, often seen as part of an ongoing celebration that starts with cleaning out all leavened products, celebrating the Pesach seder and ending with the last night of yeast-free living.

For this reason, as with HaMatzah, Bikkurim can often get overlooked or lost within the Pesach festival. But it is a Scriptural command to observe this as an individual festival in its own right, and, at risk of repeating myself, it can't be overstated how important it is to keep that fact in mind because of its part in the overall Messianic prophetic nature of all the Moedim.

You may find that the term 'first fruits' is also often associated with the celebration of Shavuot rather than that of Pesach. It is easy for the feasts of Bikkurim and Shavuot to get mixed up because they are both called feasts of first fruits.

However, reading the Scripture will clarify which of the first fruit festivals is referred to here, during the Pesach week.

The Lord said to Moses, "Tell the people of Israel, 'After you enter the land I am giving you and harvest its ripe crops, you are to bring a sheaf of the firstfruits of your harvest to the priest. He is to wave the sheaf before the Lord, so that you will be accepted; the priest is to wave it on the day after the Shabbat. Lev 23:9-11

It continues, in verses 15-16,

> *"'From the day after the day of rest — that is, from the day you bring the sheaf for waving — you are to count seven full weeks, until the day after the seventh week; you are to count fifty days; and then you are to present a new grain offering to the Lord.*

Here, the people are told to bring an offering and wave it before the Lord. Then, they are to count fifty days and bring a new offering to be waved before the Lord. The second offering of the first fruit is on Shavuot (Pentecost), which occurs seven weeks after HaBikkurim (which is why Shavuot is also called the feast of weeks). So it is clear from Scripture that there are two festivals called first fruits, not one. So, it's not surprising that there can be some confusion.

It is also an opportunity for those who don't accept Yeshua as the long-awaited and longed-for Messiah to incorporate the dates into one festival and cover over and hide the Messianic implications of the Moed. As you will see later in the book, there is another opportunity to do so again with a manufactured replacement later in the year.

The first fruit which takes place at the time of Pesach is a call to bring the first fruit of the Barley harvest. The second, at Shavuot, fifty days later, is the first fruit of wheat. The first fruits of barley and wheat are part of Jewish agricultural and religious traditions, each associated with a specific time of year. They serve as reminders of ancient Israel's agricultural cycles and have symbolic and spiritual significance in Jewish practice.

HaBikkurim is not as widely observed as a separate feast day today in traditional Judaism as are most other Jewish holidays, perhaps because of its Messianic implication. For all that, it remains an essential part of the Biblical calendar. It has profound spiritual meaning for those in both traditional and Messianic Judaism.

So, Bikkurim is the name by which the first of the first fruit festivals is known, and Shavuot is the name linked to the second first fruit festival. As I've already said, this second festival is also alternatively known as the Feast of Weeks, and we'll look closer at the details shortly.

These first fruit festivals are times to remember and thank the Lord for His provision for His people, first as they left captivity in Egypt and then as they settled in the land that He gave them.

This waving of the sheaf symbolises gratitude for and dedication of the harvest and acknowledgement of God's provision in blessing them with the bounty of the land. It is worth noting the following verse in Leviticus, chapter 23, which is something else the Lord commands of us.

"When you harvest the ripe crops produced in your land, don't harvest all the way to the corners of your field, and don't gather the ears of grain left by the harvesters; leave them for the poor and the foreigner; I am A<small>DONAI</small> your God".

Here, we have one of the basic principles of all forms of Judaism. We are told not to keep everything God has given us for ourselves. The first and best part is to be offered to God. Then we are to take what we need, and finally, we must also make provision for those in need, both for His people and the strangers living amongst us.

Leviticus 23:11 says that this first Feast of the first fruit will be celebrated on the day after the Shabbat. In other words, Scripture doesn't assign a fixed date as it does for Pesach, which is Nisan 14th and HaMatzah, which is Nisan 15th. We are only told it will be held on the first day after the Shabbat.

The problem is compounded because Leviticus 23 is unclear as to which kind of Shabbat is discussed here. Is it the standard 7th day weekly Shabbat, or is it one of those associated with the other feasts?

There was much debate and argument as to how to find a solution to this problem. Ultimately, the decision was made (for reasons we don't need to go into here) that the Shabbat of verse 11 is not the 7th day weekly Shabbat but refers to the Shabbat that is the first day of Unleavened Bread. So it has become accepted that this first fruit will occur yearly on the fixed day of Nissan 16. This aligns with the Messianic implication for this festival, as we shall see.

So, Pesach is on Nissan 14th, HaMatzot is on Nissan 15th, which is also a Shabbat day set aside for preparation, and because the Bikkurim comes on the day after the additional Shabbat, then Bikkurim is deemed to be Nissan 16th. So here we have the three consecutive Biblical Feasts of Pesach, Matzah, and Bikkurim, all connected, intertwined and celebrated almost as one event within Pesach.

Although Jewish communities worldwide generally observe the commandment and devote significant time and effort to removing all yeast products from their homes, fulfilling Biblical commands, and celebrating the Pesach Seder, the first fruit festival usually passes without much mention. While there are very few details of how it should be kept, that is also true of many of the Moedim.

In Deuteronomy 26, the command regarding giving thanks to God for His excellent provision, the reason for the festival's keeping, is outlined. Perhaps it is because so little is said about it in Scripture it doesn't get as much attention or have as many traditions attached to it as the other Moedim do.

In Yeshua's time, on this day, a sheaf (called an omer) of barley, the first of the grain crops to ripen, was waved before the Lord in a prescribed ceremony to mark the 'counting of the omer,' thereby initiating the countdown to the second first fruit ceremony, the waving of the first wheat crop on Shavuot. We'll look closer at that very soon.

Alternatively, as already stated, it could also be possible that it has been largely ignored and overlooked because of the Messianic connotations associated with the concept of first fruit, as we shall now consider.

HaBikkurim from a Messianic Jewish perspective.

At its core, Yom HaBikkurim marks the offering of the first fruits of the spring harvest to God, acknowledging His provision and sovereignty over the land. This agricultural ritual serves as a symbolic act of gratitude, recognising that the harvest is ultimately a gift from the Creator.

In the context of Messianic Judaism, the concept of first fruits is rich with Messianic implications, linking the agricultural practice to spiritual truths. In the New Testament, the connection between Yom HaBikkurim and the Messianic narrative becomes more pronounced.

For Messianic Jews, Yom HaBikkurim is a foreshadowing of the resurrection of Yeshua from the dead. The apostle Paul parallels the first fruits offering and the resurrection in 1 Corinthians 15:20-23, where Yeshua is identified as the "first fruits of those who have fallen asleep."

> *"But the fact is that the Messiah has been raised from the dead, the **first fruit** of those who have died. Since death came through a man, the resurrection of the dead has come through a man. As in connection with Adam, all die, so in connection with the Messiah, all will be made alive. But each in his own order: the Messiah is the **first fruit**; then those who belong to the Messiah, at the time of his coming."*
>
> 1 Corinthians 15:20-23 (Emphasis mine)

This symbolises His victory over death and the promise of resurrection with Him for believers. The resurrection of Yeshua, celebrated during the Passover season, aligns with the timing of Yom HaBikkurim, reinforcing the Messianic significance of this feast.

Moreover, the imagery of the barley sheaf being waved before the Lord on Yom HaBikkurim also carries profound symbolism. It represents the resurrected Messiah and the spiritual harvest of souls. Just as the first fruits offering consecrated the entire harvest, Yeshua's resurrection paves the way for the redemption of humanity, marking the beginning of the new covenant and the future outpouring of the Holy Spirit.

In Messianic Judaism, the celebration of Yom HaBikkurim is an opportunity to reflect on the interconnectedness of the physical and spiritual realms. The agricultural practices of ancient Israel become a canvas on which the Messianic message is painted, revealing God's redemptive plan through Yeshua. As believers gather to observe this feast, they not only express gratitude for the provision of the land but rejoice in the ultimate provision of salvation through the risen Messiah.

In conclusion, Yom HaBikkurim encapsulates a profound messianic message within the tapestry of agricultural rituals and biblical narratives. It bridges the Old and New Testaments, weaving together the themes of resurrection, redemption, and the spiritual harvest. For Messianic Jews, this feast is a powerful reminder of the transformative work of the Messiah and an opportunity to share the message of salvation.

9a. The Omer. Let's make the days count.

Yom HaBikkurim is the day in the Jewish calendar that signals the beginning of the countdown to the next Moed, Shavuot, also known as the Festival of Weeks or Pentecost in Greek. Celebrated on the 16th of Nisan, Yom HaBikkurm offers the barley harvest's first fruits.

This day also marks the start of the Omer count, as outlined in Leviticus 23:15-16, which lasts 49 days, beginning from the second day of Passover and culminating on Shavuot. During this period, the Jewish community counts each day in anticipation of Shavuot.

Yom HaBikkurim starts the grain harvest season with the barley offering and initiates a period of preparation for the more significant wheat harvest, celebrated at Shavuot. The Omer counting is a literal countdown and a spiritual journey involving reflection, personal growth, and spiritual refinement.

This period prepares the community for Shavuot, a time to commemorate the giving of the Torah at Mount Sinai. The transition from Yom HaBikkurim to Shavuot reflects the physical journey from barley to wheat harvest and the spiritual journey from the Exodus during Passover to the reception of the Torah at Shavuot.

In Messianic Judaism, these observances take on additional significance. The Omer counting, traditionally a time of introspection and anticipation of the Torah, also symbolises awaiting the Holy Spirit's outpouring. Shavuot is significant for followers of Yeshua, commemorating, as it does, the Holy Spirit being bestowed upon the disciples, fulfilling God's promise to all believers.

In summary, Yom HaBikkurim connects the Passover to Shavuot through the Omer count, signifying the transition from the initial barley offering to the completion of the wheat harvest. This period mirrors a spiritual journey towards receiving the Torah and the Holy Spirit, holding profound meaning in traditional Jewish and Messianic traditions as a time of spiritual growth and strengthening our connection with God, completing another step in God's fantastic Messianic plan of redemption and salvation.

Chapter 10.

Shavuot - Pentecost.

Dairy Delight on Torah Night.

The feast of Shavuot, known in Christianity as Pentecost, comes after the counting of the omer, seven weeks after HaBikkurim. Therefore, it also carries the title of the feast of weeks. It is one of the pilgrimage festivals in Judaism, along with Hamatzot and Sukkot. These are festivals when as many as were able made the journey to the temple in Yerushalayim to offer sacrifices in the Temple and to celebrate. It marks the beginning of the wheat harvest.

In addition to the grain offering, specific instructions on making sacrifices are linked to this festival. These were to be done by the priests in the Temple following the instructions found in Leviticus 23:15-20.

The Temple in Yerushalayim held paramount significance as the exclusive and sacred venue for conducting religious sacrifices. This temple, revered and central to the religious practices of the time, served as the focal point for such rituals.

However, a pivotal moment in history occurred with the demolition of the Second Temple by Roman forces in the year 70 CE. This event marked a profound turning point, as it left the Jewish people without a suitable and consecrated location for carrying out these traditional sacrificial rites.

Shavuot, originally an agricultural festival, is rooted in the ancient Israelite practice of bringing the first fruits of the harvest to the Temple in Yerushalayim as an offering to God. This aspect of Shavuot is deeply connected to the land of Israel and its agricultural cycles. The festival's timing, precisely seven weeks after Pesach, links it to the beginning of the grain harvest, marking a period of abundance. In this context, Shavuot celebrates God's provision and bounty, reminding the Jewish people of their dependence on and gratitude to God for the fruits of the earth.

Beyond its agricultural significance, Shavuot assumes a monumental spiritual dimension as it commemorates the giving of the Torah at Mount Sinai. According to Scripture, on this day, fifty days after their exodus from Egypt, the Israelites gathered at the foot of Mount Sinai to receive the Torah, the central text and very foundation of Judaism. This event is the foundational moment in Jewish history, establishing the covenant between God and the Israelite people and shaping their identity as a nation bound by divine law.

The Torah, comprising the first five books of the Hebrew Bible, is more than a legal code; it is a comprehensive guide to ethical and spiritual living, a source of wisdom and moral instruction. The giving of the Torah is therefore celebrated as a moment of divine revelation, when God chose to communicate directly with humanity, entrusting them with the responsibilities of His teachings.

The customs and traditions of Shavuot reflect its dual agricultural and spiritual character. One of the most notable customs is reading the Book of Ruth. This biblical story, set during the harvest season, tells of Ruth, a Moabite woman who converts to Judaism and becomes the great-grandmother of King David. Her story of loyalty, conversion, and redemption resonates with the themes of Shavuot, underscoring the universal appeal of the Torah and the inclusivity of the Jewish faith.

One of the telling moments in the story of Ruth is God's commandment concerning leaving some crops at the edge of the field, as previously explained. If that hadn't been commanded in Scripture, if the land owner, Boaz, had disobeyed or if Ruth hadn't collected some of it, she would, in all likelihood, never have become the grandmother of King David from whose line Yeshua came. This is another beautiful example of the intricacy of God's unique plan of salvation.

A significant tradition is the all-night study of Torah, known as Tikkun Leil Shavuot. This practice involves communal gatherings where people study Biblical texts, discuss Jewish philosophy, and engage in spiritual contemplation. This tradition stems from the mystical belief that the Israelites overslept the night before receiving the Torah. To atone for this, Jews stay awake all night to study and show their eagerness to receive the Torah.

Shavuot is also characterised by decorating homes and synagogues with greenery and flowers, symbolising the spring harvest and Mount Sinai's beauty during the Torah's giving.

In addition, it is customary to eat dairy foods during Shavuot, cheesecake being one of the favourites. Various explanations exist for this tradition, including the idea that upon receiving the Torah, the Israelites did not have time to prepare kosher meat, so they ate dairy instead. (That suits me as I have a weakness for a delicious cheesecake).

Shavuot remains a highly relevant festival in contemporary Jewish life. It serves as a yearly reminder of the Jewish people's historical and spiritual journey, from the liberation of Pesach to the revelation of Shavuot. This progression from physical freedom to spiritual enlightenment encapsulates a fundamental Jewish belief: true freedom is embracing divine law and ethical living.

Moreover, Shavuot's emphasis on Torah study highlights the value placed on education and intellectual engagement in Judaism. The tradition of Tikkun Leil Shavuot embodies the Jewish commitment to lifelong learning and the continual reinterpretation of religious texts in light of changing times and contexts.

In a broader sense, Shavuot offers a moment of reflection on the nature of revelation and the human-divine relationship. It invites Jews to consider the ongoing relevance of ancient teachings in modern life and to recommit themselves to the principles and values enshrined in the Torah.

Shavuot is a festival of great depth and richness, encompassing themes of gratitude, revelation, and renewal. It celebrates the dual blessings of physical sustenance and spiritual guidance, linking the agricultural cycles of the land of Israel with the pivotal moment of divine revelation at Mount Sinai.

Through its customs and traditions, Shavuot reinforces the centrality of the Torah in Jewish life, underscoring the importance of learning, ethical conduct, and a deep connection to one's heritage. As a time of historical remembrance and contemporary reflection, Shavuot continues to resonate with Jews worldwide, reminding them of their roots and inspiring them to live according to their most cherished beliefs and values.

Shavuot from a Messianic Jewish perspective.

Shavuot holds a significant place in the Messianic Jewish perspective. It marks the end of the Counting of the Omer, 49 days of reflection and spiritual preparation beginning after Pesach, HaMatzah and HaBikkurim. Historically, it celebrates the harvest season in Israel and the giving of the Torah at Mount Sinai. In Exodus 19, the Israelites arrived at Sinai, and in Exodus 20, God gave the Ten Commandments. This moment is pivotal in Jewish history, signifying the covenant between God and Israel.

In Messianic Judaism, Shavuot is a celebration enriched with deep significance. It not only honours the giving of the Torah but also marks the fulfilment of biblical prophecy through the coming of the Holy Spirit, an event depicted in the New Testament's Book of Acts. This pivotal moment, where the Holy Spirit descended upon Yeshua's disciples in Yerushalayim, is the realisation of the new covenant promised in Jeremiah 31:31-34 - written on hearts of flesh rather than stone tablets.

As previously stated (Chapter 5a, pages 55-56), Shavuot, Pentecost, does not represent the church's birth.

For Messianic Jews, Shavuot is a time to commemorate the Torah's delivery and the gift of the Spirit, made possible through Yeshua's life, death, and resurrection. This connection underscores a significant shift from the physical laws given to Moses to the spiritual laws instilled in believers' hearts, highlighting a central theme in their theology: the law's transformation from stone to flesh.

The festival does not merely look back; it also celebrates the present understanding of God's teachings through the lens of the New Testament. The Holy Spirit, received during this time, empowers followers to embody the Torah's moral and ethical instructions more profoundly and personally. This view doesn't replace the Torah but enriches and completes it, illustrating the complementary nature of the Old and New Testaments in Messianic thought.

Traditional practices are woven into Messianic Jewish Shavuot observances, often including studying the Torah, reading the Book of Ruth, and enjoying dairy foods. The story of Ruth holds special significance as it symbolises the inclusive nature of God's salvation, available to both Jews and Gentiles - a fundamental belief in Messianic Judaism.

Moreover, modern celebrations may feature worship services that blend traditional Jewish prayers with Messianic praise music, emphasising the Holy Spirit's role and celebrating the unity among Jewish and Gentile believers in Yeshua.

Shavuot allows Messianic Jews to reflect on their unique identity, merging their belief in Yeshua as the Messiah with their Jewish heritage. It's a festival commemorating God's enduring faithfulness, from the Torah's revelation to the Holy Spirit's arrival. It offers a rich, multifaceted celebration that bridges the testamentary divide and underscores the Messianic promise of universal salvation and spiritual renewal.

"Do not say, 'when I am free of my concerns, I will study,' for perhaps you will never free yourself." Pirkot Avot 2:4

This quote, often associated with Shavuot, underscores the continuous commitment to Torah study, which is central to the festival's celebrations.

Chapter 11.

Yom Teruah - Blowing of the shofar.

God told Moses, "Tell the people of Israel, 'In the seventh month, the first of the month is to be for you a day of complete rest for remembering, a holy convocation announced with blasts on the shofar. Do not do any kind of ordinary work, and bring an offering made by fire to God.'"

Leviticus 23:23-25

As previously mentioned, Scripture often offers very little detail about how to mark and celebrate each Moed, and this is all Scripture says about Yom Teruah. It is to be a Shabbat; we are to gather to hear the blowing of the Shofar, a trumpet made from an animal's horn, and bring an offering made by fire. That's all it tells us, but as with the other Moedim, how we should mark it and what we should do to celebrate it has been discussed and debated over the millennia.

So, originally, this was primarily a day for the sounding of the shofar, which served various purposes in ancient Israel, such as calling assemblies, signalling war, and marking significant events.

But today, in traditional Judaism, Yom Teruah is known as Rosh Hashanah, which means 'head of the year', and it has become a significant festival in Jewish tradition. Its evolution from a purely and simply described biblical commandment to blow the shofar into a ceremony marking the Jewish New Year is a long journey through history, culture, and religious interpretation.

Understanding this transformation requires us to look briefly at ancient scriptures, cultural shifts, and the evolving nature of Jewish religious practices.

In the Torah, specifically in the book of Leviticus (23:23-25), we find this festival mentioned, and the original purpose of Yom

Teruah seems to have been more about creating a sacred time for reflection and spiritual awakening, signalled by the piercing sound of the shofar, than of a new year starting.

The shift from Yom Teruah to Rosh Hashanah as the Jewish New Year is not well-documented historically but is believed to have occurred during the 6th century BCE amidst the Babylonian exile. Influenced by the Babylonian Akitu festival, a pagan New Year celebration, it's possible that the Jewish people changed Yom Teruah (Day of the Shofar) into Rosh Hashanah (New Year) to resonate with the local customs. The Torah identifies Nisan, typically in March or April, as the start of the year (Exodus 12:2), marking the Israelites' exodus from Egypt. However, the calendar was later revised to designate Tishrei as the first month.

The term "Rosh Hashanah" first appears in the Mishnah, compiled around 200 CE, signifying its full acceptance as the New Year by the early Common Era.

The Mishnah highlights Rosh Hashanah as a day of judgment, evaluating the deeds of individuals. Over time, Jewish scholars began to associate the day with the creation of Adam and Eve, thereby broadening its significance to encompass all humanity, underscoring themes of creation, renewal, and kingship. Rosh Hashanah's observance evolved to include traditions and liturgy, reflecting its position as the New Year.

The shofar remains pivotal, calling for repentance and acknowledging God's reign. Unique prayers mark the holiday, and readings focus on judgement and remembrance alongside practices such as eating apples dipped in honey to express hopes for a prosperous year.

It begins the Ten Days of Repentance, also known as the Days of Awe, culminating in Yom Kippur, the Day of Atonement. This period is a time for reflection, self-examination, and seeking forgiveness. The transformation of Yom Teruah into Rosh

Hashanah thus reflects a deepening of the spiritual and moral dimensions of the Jewish faith. It's not just the start of a new year; it's a call to renew one's relationship with God and others.

The holiday is also seen as a time when God inscribes each person's fate for the coming year into the "Book of Life" or the "Book of Death." This belief emphasises the importance of repentance, prayer, and charity during Rosh Hashanah to influence God's judgement.

The evolution of Yom Teruah into Rosh Hashanah is a fascinating example of how religious practices and interpretations can change over time. While the Torah laid the foundation, the Jewish people's experiences and historical circumstances significantly shaped the holiday as we know it today. With its blend of ancient ritual and evolved meaning, Rosh Hashanah continues to be a vital part of Jewish life and spirituality.

In conclusion, Yom Teruah's journey to becoming Rosh Hashanah illustrates the dynamic nature of religious traditions. It shows how festivals and rituals can adapt to new contexts and acquire deeper layers of meaning.

However, this is often be done without any Scriptural support, sometimes even going against what God's Word says. Occasionally, as in this instance, it can done to be more conforming with outside influences and cultural differences and to avoid confrontation and persecution.

While the biblical new year in Exodus marks a historical and seasonal beginning, the new year for the kings and festivals, Rosh Hashanah, represents a spiritual and moral renewal and has become associated with the world's creation.

Yom Teruah from a Messianic Jewish perspective.

Yom Teruah is a significant Jewish holiday with profound spiritual meaning, especially from a Messianic perspective. So, let's explore the Messianic aspects of Yom Teruah to see how they relate to the belief in the Messiah.

In Judaism, Yom Teruah, or Rosh Hashanah, is traditionally observed as the Jewish New Year and also marks the beginning of the High Holy Days, a ten-day period of introspection and repentance, known as the days of awe, that culminates in Yom Kippur.

This holiday is characterised by the blowing of the shofar, a ram's horn, which serves as a call to self-examination, repentance, and renewal. In the Bible, specifically in Leviticus 23:24 and Numbers 29:1, Yom Teruah is mandated as a day of rest, a memorial with the blowing of trumpets, and a holy convocation.

From a Messianic perspective, viewing Jewish traditions with the belief in Yeshua as the Messiah, Yom Teruah is imbued with deeper meanings. The shofar blowing, an essential practice during this holiday, symbolises themes at the heart of Messianic faith.

Primarily, it acts as an alert to believers, emphasising the need for spiritual readiness for the Messiah's arrival, a figure prophesied to bring global peace and harmony.

Additionally, the shofar's call is linked to the resurrection of the dead, a shared belief in Jewish and Messianic teachings, signalling the momentous time when the dead shall rise at the Messiah's coming. This concept is supported by biblical passages, including Isaiah, Daniel, and 1 Thessalonians, which speak of the dead being awakened to life.

But your dead will live; their bodies will rise - let those who dwell in the dust wake up and shout for joy - your dew is like the dew of the morning; the earth will give birth to her dead.
Isaiah 26:19

Multitudes who sleep in the dust of the earth will awake: some to everlasting life, others to shame and everlasting contempt.
Daniel 12:2

The Lord Himself will come down from heaven with a rousing cry, a call from one of the ruling angels, and with God's shofar, and those who died united with the Messiah will be the first to rise.
1 Thessalonians 4:16

Furthermore, Yom Teruah is a time of reflection on judgement, renewal, and God's sovereignty. It is a day when, according to tradition, God examines the Book of Life to decide each person's fate, reflecting the Messianic anticipation of a final judgement. The ten days following Yom Teruah, leading to Yom Kippur, are seen as an opportunity for repentance and reconciliation.

The holiday also marks the beginning of a new agricultural cycle, symbolising fresh starts and the hope for personal and global renewal. This aligns with the Messianic vision of a future era of peace as prophesied in scriptures like Isaiah 11 and Zechariah 14:9, which foretell God's ultimate reign.

Leopards will lie down with young goats, and wolves will rest with lambs. Calves and lions will eat together and be led by little children. Cows and bears will share the same pasture; their young will rest side by side. Lions and oxen will both eat straw. Little children will play near snake holes. They will stick their hands into dens of poisonous snakes and never be hurt. Nothing harmful will take place on the Lord's holy mountain. Just as water fills the sea, the land will be filled with people who know and honour the Lord.
Isaiah 11:6-9.

The Lord will be king over the whole earth. On that day, there will be one Lord, whose name will be the only name.   Zechariah 14:9

In summary, Yom Teruah for Messianic believers is not just a traditional observance but a profound spiritual reflection and anticipation period. The shofar's blast serves as a multifaceted symbol, calling for awareness, symbolising resurrection, and heralding divine judgement and kingship. It invites believers to introspect and look forward to the Messiah's reign and the fulfilment of prophecies, giving the holiday a unique and significant place in the Messianic calendar.

'On Rosh HaShanah, all beings will pass before Him.' Mishnah, Rosh HaShanah 1:2

This quote refers to the belief that on Rosh HaShanah (Yom Teruah), all beings are judged by God like a shepherd counting His sheep.

Chapter 12.

Yom Kippur - Day of Atonement.

Yom Kippur, also known as the Day of Atonement, is the holiest day in all streams of Judaism. It is a time for reflection, prayer, and repentance. It falls on the 10th day of Tishrei, the seventh month of the Hebrew Biblical calendar and marks the culmination of ten days of introspection and repentance known as the Days of Awe, which begins with Yom Teruah.

The origins of Yom Kippur can be traced back to the biblical story of Moses. After the Israelites sinned by worshipping the Golden Calf, Moses interceded on their behalf with God. According to Jewish tradition, God forgave the Israelites on the tenth day of the month of Tishrei, which became Yom Kippur. This day thus symbolises God's willingness to forgive repentant sinners.

It's mentioned in several Hebrew Scriptures, primarily in the Torah. Here are key sources where you can find details about Yom Kippur:

Leviticus 16: This is the primary and most detailed source about Yom Kippur in the Torah. It describes the rituals performed by the High Priest in the Temple, including the sacrifice of a goat and the sending away of a second goat (the "scapegoat") into the wilderness, symbolising the removal of the people's sins.

Leviticus 23:26-32: This section outlines the timing of Yom Kippur, marking it as a day of solemn rest, fasting, and self-denial, occurring on the 10th day of the seventh month (Tishrei) on the Jewish calendar.

Numbers 29:7-11: This passage mentions the additional offerings in the Temple on Yom Kippur, including a sin offering to atone for the High Priest and the community.

Isaiah 58: While not explicitly mentioning Yom Kippur, this chapter is often associated with the holiday. It discusses the true meaning of fasting and calls for social justice and the ethical treatment of others, central to Yom Kippur.

The significance of Yom Kippur is multifaceted. It is a day dedicated to personal introspection, spiritual cleansing, and reconciliation with God and fellow human beings. The central themes of the day are atonement and repentance. Jews traditionally observe this holy day with 25 hours of fasting and intensive prayer. The fast begins at sunset on the eve of Yom Kippur and ends after nightfall on the day of Yom Kippur.

The fast is not merely a physical discipline but is meant to be a spiritual cleansing. By abstaining from the physical comfort of partaking in meals, individuals can focus entirely on their spiritual selves, praying, and repentance.

Prayer is central to the observance of Yom Kippur, and services are held throughout the day in synagogues, where congregants engage in intense supplication and confession of sins. The prayers on Yom Kippur are unique and include liturgical pieces specific to the day.

One of the most significant prayers is the "Kol Nidre," recited at the beginning of the Yom Kippur evening service. "Kol Nidre" is a prayer for annulling all vows made during the past year, symbolically freeing individuals from past obligations and allowing them to start anew.

Another significant aspect of Yom Kippur prayer is the confession of sins, known as "Vidui." This is a communal confession, where the congregation recites a litany of sins together. The communal aspect of this confession is essential; it acknowledges that all individuals are flawed and in need of atonement, fostering a sense of unity and shared responsibility within the community.

Its focus on reconciliation and forgiveness also characterises Yom

Kippur. It is a common belief that Yom Kippur atones only for sins between a person and God. For sins against another person, Yom Kippur cannot atone until one has first sought to reconcile with the person they have wronged and made amends. This aspect underscores the importance of human relationships in Jewish ethics and the belief that interpersonal harmony is crucial for a truly meaningful life.

The day concludes with the "Neilah" service, which means "closing." This service represents the closing of the gates of heaven, the last chance to repent before the day ends. The conclusion of Neilah is marked by a single long blast of the shofar, a ram's horn, signalling the end of the fast. This powerful and emotional sound signifies a spiritual release and a hopeful start to the new year. A light communal meal, usually soup, is enjoyed together at the end of the day to break the day's fast.

Yom Kippur's impact extends beyond religious observance. It has significant cultural and social implications. In Israel, for example, the day is observed by most of the population, including many who do not consider themselves religious. Streets are empty of cars, and people, regardless of their level of observance, are dressed in white as a symbol of purity. The atmosphere in the country is one of solemnity and reflection, creating a unique sense of national unity and shared purpose.

The philosophical and ethical teachings of Yom Kippur have a universal appeal. The emphasis on introspection, the admission of one's faults, the importance of forgiveness, and the striving for a better self resonate with many, regardless of their religious background. These themes are universal in their appeal and offer valuable lessons for people of all faiths.

In summary, Yom Kippur is a day of great solemnity and profound spirituality in Judaism. It is a day for atonement, repentance, and reconciliation. The traditions and observances of Yom Kippur, such as fasting, prayer, and the confession of sins, serve to guide individuals in their spiritual journey, encouraging them to reflect on their actions, seek forgiveness, and strive for a better and more meaningful life. The day's emphasis on ethical living, community responsibility, and the pursuit of harmony makes its teachings relevant not only to Jews but to people of all backgrounds, offering a moment each year for profound spiritual renewal and moral reflection.

Yom Kippur from a Messianic Jewish perspective.

From a Messianic Judaism perspective, this day, in addition to being marked by intense reflection, prayer, and fasting, takes on an additional layer of significance as it is seen through the lens of Yeshua HaMashiach.

Yom Kippur is the culmination of the Ten Days of Repentance that begins with Yom Teruah. This period is a time for self-examination and repentance, a spiritual journey that leads to Yom Kippur.

In traditional Judaism, this day is set aside to atone for the sins of the past year. However, this day takes on a new dimension in Messianic Judaism as believers reflect on their sins and the atonement provided through Yeshua.

Messianic Jews observe Yom Kippur like other Jewish communities, with fasting and prayer but with an added emphasis on Yeshua as the ultimate atonement for sin.

The central theme of Yom Kippur in the Torah is the High Priest entering the Holy of Holies to make atonement for the people of Israel. In Leviticus 16, the High Priest performs elaborate rituals to cleanse himself and the people from their sins.

Messianic Jews see these rituals as a foreshadowing of Yeshua's sacrifice. They believe that just as the High Priest made atonement for the sins of Israel, Yeshua, the ultimate High Priest, made atonement possible for the sins of all humanity through his death and resurrection.

This perspective transforms the observance of Yom Kippur. While the day is still a solemn time of repentance, it is also viewed as a time of gratitude for the atonement already achieved by Yeshua. Messianic Jews spend the day in prayer and reflection, but their focus is on thanking God for the forgiveness and redemption granted through Yeshua. This does not mean they take sin lightly or feel that repentance is unnecessary. On the contrary, they see their belief in Yeshua as a call to a higher standard of holiness and ethical living.

Messianic Jews often reference the book of Hebrews in the New Testament during Yom Kippur. Hebrews describes Yeshua as the High Priest who did not enter a man-made sanctuary but heaven itself to appear for humanity before God.

This view sees Yeshua's sacrifice as fulfilling and surpassing the sacrificial system of the Old Testament. In this light, Yom Kippur becomes a day to remember the atonement and celebrate Yeshua's new covenant, offering a direct relationship with God and forgiveness of sins.

Fasting on Yom Kippur, for Messianic Jews, is not just an act of penitence but also an expression of humility and dependence on God. It is a physical reminder of the spiritual truth that they do not live on bread alone but on every word that comes from the mouth of God, as Yeshua quotes from Deuteronomy during his temptation in the wilderness. Some also see the fast as a way to identify with the suffering of Yeshua, who fasted for 40 days and nights in the desert.

Yom Kippur is also a time for Messianic Jews to pray for the peace of Yerushalayim and all Israel. They often include prayers for the Jewish people to recognise Yeshua as the Messiah. This is not meant triumphally or coercively but rather as an expression of their belief in the prophetic destiny of all Israel and the Jewish people. In conclusion, from a Messianic Judaism perspective, Yom Kippur is a day steeped in the traditions of Judaism, yet viewed through the belief in Yeshua as the Messiah.

It is a day of repentance, reflection, fasting, and gratitude for the atonement and redemption offered through Yeshua, the Messiah.

This perspective adds a unique dimension to the observance of Yom Kippur, blending traditional Jewish practice with the beliefs of the New Testament. As such, it embodies the dual identity of Messianic Jews as both adherents of Judaism and believers in Yeshua as the Messiah.

"For on this day He will forgive you, to purify you, that you may be cleansed from all your sin before God." Leviticus 16:30

Chapter 13.

Sukkot - Tabernacles / Booths.

Intense times living in tents.

Sukkot, also known as the Feast of Tabernacles or Booths, is a significant Jewish festival celebrated at the end of the annual cycle of Moedim. It is a time of joy and gratitude, commemorating the Israelites' journey through the wilderness after their exodus from Egypt and their reliance on the protection of God, who came and dwelt or tabernacled with them.

The festival lasts seven days in Israel and eight days in the diaspora, beginning on the 15th day of the Hebrew month of Tishrei, which usually falls in late September or October.

"Sukkot" is derived from the Hebrew word "sukkah," meaning booth or tabernacle. During this festival, it is customary for Jews to build and dwell in temporary shelters, symbolising the fragile and transient nature of life and recalling the temporary shelters the Israelites lived in during their 40 years in the desert.

The sukkah is often beautifully decorated with fruits, vegetables, and other natural materials, creating a festive and welcoming atmosphere. When constructing the sukkah, it is customary to use branches for the roof, ensuring the night sky and the stars, where light pollution allows, are visible through the gaps.

One of the most important aspects of Sukkot is the concept of hospitality. This tradition involves inviting living and spiritual guests into the sukkah. It is often believed that a different biblical figure symbolically joins the gathering each night, adding a spiritual dimension to the physical act of hospitality. This custom emphasises the values of generosity, community, and inclusiveness central to Jewish tradition.

Another critical component of Sukkot is the Four Species, or "Arba Minim" in Hebrew. The four plants mentioned in the Torah are the etrog (citron), lulav (palm frond), hadass (myrtle), and aravah (willow). These species are bound together and waved in all directions during the Sukkot prayers, symbolising the recognition of God's omnipresence and the unity of the Jewish people.

With its taste and aroma, the etrog represents those who study Torah and perform good deeds. The lulav, with taste but no smell, symbolises those who study Torah but do not perform deeds. The hadass, with a pleasant aroma but no taste, represents those who perform good deeds but do not study Torah. The aravah, having neither taste nor smell, symbolises those who lack both Torah study and good deeds. Together, they represent the unity and diversity within the Jewish community.

Sukkot is not only a time of historical remembrance but also has agricultural significance. It coincides with the end of the harvest season in Israel and is a time to give thanks for the earth's bounty. This aspect of Sukkot connects it to the universal theme of gratitude for nature's gifts, making it a festival with both national and universal significance.

Throughout the week of Sukkot, meals are eaten in the sukkah, and some people even sleep there, weather permitting. In parts of the world where the weather makes it impractical to have their sukkah outdoors, a smaller sukkah is often built and utilised inside the main living area. The sukkah thus becomes a place of gathering, eating, studying, and celebrating, filled with the joy of the festival. Special prayers, including the Hallel, a series of psalms praising God, are recited.

The seventh day of Sukkot is known as Hoshana Rabbah. On this day, a particular service is held in which worshippers often circle the synagogue seven times while holding the Four Species and reciting prayers for salvation. This day is considered the final judgement day for the year's agricultural yield and, by extension, a symbolic judgement for the year ahead.

In essence, Sukkot serves as a reminder of the transient nature of life and the importance of relying on something greater than oneself. The sukkah's fragile structure symbolises life's vulnerability, yet it also represents protection and divine presence. Leaving the comfort of one's home to dwell in the sukkah is a physical manifestation of faith and trust in God's protection, just as the Israelites did in the desert.

The festival's emphasis on hospitality extends beyond welcoming guests into one's sukkah; it is also about opening one's heart and extending kindness and generosity to others, especially those less fortunate. This spirit of inclusiveness and community is at the heart of Sukkot. It is when barriers are broken down, and people come together in a shared space, emphasising unity and mutual support.

The Four Species, with their diverse characteristics, not only symbolise different types of people but also remind us of the importance of unity in diversity. Waving them in all directions signifies recognition of God's sovereignty over all creation and the interconnectedness of all life.

The agricultural aspect of Sukkot is particularly relevant in today's context of environmental consciousness. The festival's connection to the harvest season serves as a reminder of humanity's dependence on the natural world and the need to live in harmony with it. It is a time to appreciate the earth's bounty and to acknowledge our responsibility to care for the environment.

Sukkot continues to evolve in contemporary Jewish practice, with newer traditions and interpretations enriching its observance. It remains a vibrant and dynamic festival deeply rooted in Jewish history and tradition. It speaks to universal themes of gratitude, hospitality, environmental stewardship, and the search for meaning in our transient world.

In conclusion, Sukkot is a festival with deep significance for the Jewish people. It is a time of joy, reflection, and community, inviting participants to engage with faith, gratitude, unity, and environmental consciousness. By dwelling in the sukkah, welcoming guests, and celebrating the bounty of the harvest, Jews around the world reconnect with their heritage and the timeless lessons of their ancestors. Sukkot thus stands as a powerful symbol of faith, resilience, and the enduring spirit of the Jewish people.

Sukkot from a Messianic Jewish perspective.

Messianic Jews's observation of the Sukkot festival parallels traditional Judaism's customs and traditions, with a deep gratitude for God's Divine provision and protection. This celebration is a time to acknowledge God's presence with His people and guidance during their time in the wilderness and is celebrated as a time of great joy.

Messianic Jews, like their traditional Jewish counterparts, construct Sukkahs – temporary shelters reminiscent of those used by the Israelites during their 40 years of desert wandering – as a physical representation of God's sheltering presence.

The festival is marked by gatherings within these Sukkahs, where prayers are offered and meals are shared, all in remembrance of God's enduring faithfulness and mercy. This period of reflection and thanksgiving not only honours the historical journey of the Israelites but also celebrates the continued relationship and covenant between God and His people, highlighting the spiritual significance of God dwelling among them.

However, Messianic Judaism celebrates Sukkot as more than just a historical event; it's a time of reflection on God's past, present, and future actions. This festival is not only a reminder of God providing for His people during their journey from Egypt but also looks forward to the anticipated Messianic Kingdom. The rituals and symbols during Sukkot are significant, pointing to spiritual truths and the importance of Yeshua in these celebrations.

As we have seen, each biblical festival, or moed, commemorates an important event while delivering a prophetic message. Sukkot is significant as it celebrates God's presence with His people in the wilderness and prophesies His return.

This aligns with the prophetic words from Isaiah 7:14, which speaks of a virgin giving birth to a son who will be called Immanuel, meaning "God with us." Believers see this as a reference to Yeshua's birth.

The pattern of prophecy fulfilment on specific moedim suggests that just as significant events in Yeshua's life occurred on these festivals, His return will also coincide with them.

The moedim passages highlight the deep connection between Scriptural commemorations and their prophetic fulfilment. We have observed that the pivotal moments of Yeshua's life - His death, triumph over sin, and resurrection - coincided precisely with Pesach, HaMatzah, and HaBikkurim, respectively.

Similarly, just as we commemorate the Torah being inscribed on stone tablets, we recognise that, on Shavuot, the Holy Spirit was given to us so that the law would be written upon our hearts. This illustrates how the first four moedim memorialising past events found their prophesied fulfilment when the moed was kept.

If that pattern is repeated, and we know that our God is consistent in His promises, then we can be confident that he will return with the sound of the shofar of Yom Teruah and bring judgment on the day of repentance, Yom Kippur.

But what about Sukkot? How does this fit in with God's timetable? Is the celebration of God dwelling amongst his people a foretelling of His return on Sukkot?

The traditional date of December 25th for celebrating Yeshua's birth raises questions, as it doesn't reflect the actual timing of His birth. The early Church chose this date to coincide with Roman pagan festivals, like Saturnalia and Sol Invictus, to make Christianity more appealing to Roman converts. This strategy was part of a broader effort to Christianize popular pagan festivals.

The choice of December 25th was also influenced by calculations based on biblical events. It became standardised in the 4th century AD, although different Christian communities initially celebrated Jesus' birth on various dates.

The decision to adopt December 25th reflects human reasoning and attempts to integrate Christian celebrations with existing cultural practices. This contrasts with the prophetic nature of biblical festivals, which are divinely ordained.

Sukkot, in particular, symbolises God's dwelling among His people and looks forward to Yeshua's return to rule. This leaves us with a choice: to follow human-devised dates and reasoning or to consider the consistency and detail in God's plan as revealed through Scripture, including His timetable for redemption.

For many Messianic Jews, Sukkot is the time to commemorate Yeshua's birth. Still, they do it without turning it into the commercial-driven, often multi-week pressurised occasions we so frequently witness, not just in the church but also among non-believers. It is a time of joy and celebrations as we commemorate His birth and look forward to His coming again to dwell among us, just as He did in the past.

This leaves many believers with a choice: we can follow human-devised dates and reasoning or turn to God's Word and accept the remarkable consistency and fantastic detail in His plan as revealed through the Scriptural Moedim, which includes the extraordinary timetable, commemorating the past and prophesying the future, that he has given us.

While the following two commemorations are not found in Scripture, they are celebrated as part of Sukkot in all strands of Judaism and come at the end of the festivities. Therefore, as they are considered part of Sukkot, I have included them here.

Shemini Atzeret.

Shemini Atzeret, meaning "the assembly of the eighth day," is a separate yet connected holiday that follows immediately after the seven days of Sukkot. It is a time of reflection and spiritual connection, marked by reciting a special prayer for rain, highlighting the dependence on divine grace for the year's water supply.

Simchat Torah.

Simchat Torah, or "Rejoicing of the Torah," marks the conclusion of the annual cycle of Torah readings and the beginning of a new cycle. It is a joyous celebration where the Torah scrolls are taken out of the ark and paraded around the synagogue in seven circuits, called hakafot, with singing, dancing, and flag-waving.

The Torah scroll is often passed from person to person, enabling the congregation to embrace and carry the scroll individually for part of each circuit. This celebration highlights the central role of the Torah in Jewish life and the joy of fulfilling its commandments.

From a Messianic perspective, Sukkot, Shemini Atzeret, and Simchat Torah are significant feasts that symbolise God's provision, faithfulness, and joy in His Word. They celebrate the harvest and God's sheltering presence while looking forward to the ultimate redemption and rejoicing in the Messiah. These festivals are embraced as times of thanksgiving, reflection, and anticipation of the Messiah's return, embodying both historical significance and prophetic fulfilment.

"The end of the Torah is joined to its beginning, and it's beginning to its end." Midrash Tanchuma.

This quote reflects the Torah reading cycle that concludes and begins again on Simchat Torah, symbolising the continuous, eternal nature of Torah study.

"On Sukkot, we are commanded to be joyful." Sukkah 48b

Chapter 14.

The conclusion to the Moedim from a traditional Jewish perspective.

As we reach the end of our journey, looking at the Moedim from a **traditional Jewish** perspective, we are left with a picture of how history, faith, and profound meaning transcend time and place. Each festival, a thread in the fabric of Jewish life, links the past with the present, inviting every generation to partake in the ongoing story of the Jewish people.

The Moedim are not mere commemorations; they are vibrant, living experiences that engage the Jewish community in remembrance, thanksgiving and anticipation. From the liberating echoes of Passover to the solemn introspection of Yom Kippur, these sacred times offer a unique lens through which to view the relationship between God and His people.

Pesach stands as the cornerstone of Jewish collective memory. It's a time when families gather to retell the story of Exodus, reminding us of the enduring power of freedom and the relentless spirit of a people pursuing their destiny. Matzah's unleavened bread symbolises both the haste of departure from Egypt and the purity of a faith unadulterated by the leaven of oppression. First fruit provides us the opportunity to give thanks to our maker for all his provisions.

Shavuot, marking the giving of the Torah at Sinai, invites Jews to embrace the covenant anew, reflecting on the Torah's timeless wisdom and role as a guide in their daily lives. It is a celebration of revelation, where the divine meets the human in a moment of unparalleled intimacy.

Yom Teruah awakens the soul with the blast of the Shofar, calling for a renewed commitment to God and one another. Yom Kippur, the Day of Atonement, is the culmination of this period of soul-searching, offering a chance for reconciliation and renewal.

With its fragile dwellings, Sukkot reminds us of life's transient nature and God's enduring protection. It's a festival of joy and gratitude, celebrating God's provision and care during the Israelites' wilderness journey. The Sukkah, a temporary hut, symbolises faith amid life's uncertainties.

These festivals, with their rituals, foods, and prayers, are not just historical reenactments but are imbued with contemporary relevance. They provide a framework for personal and communal growth to cultivate qualities such as gratitude, humility, and perseverance. The Moedim serve as waypoints in life's journey, guiding the Jewish community in their collective and individual pursuit of righteousness, justice, and spiritual growth.

Moreover, the Moedim are a testament to the enduring covenant between God and the Jewish people. They reinforce the identity and continuity of the Jewish community, bridging generations through shared traditions and stories. In celebrating these festivals, Jews reaffirm their place within a story that stretches back to the dawn of their history, a story filled with challenges and triumphs, exile and return, despair and hope.

As we conclude this exploration of the Moedim within traditional Judaism, it becomes clear that the Moedim are far more than historical commemorations; they are vibrant expressions of faith, hope, and resilience. They capture the essence of Jewish identity and faith, serving as a compass guiding the community through the seasons of the year and the seasons of life.

In a world that often seems disconnected from its spiritual moorings, the Moedim offer a grounding presence, a reminder of the enduring values and eternal truths that have sustained the Jewish people through millennia. They challenge each individual to reflect, celebrate, and aspire towards a deeper, more meaningful relationship with God and one another.

As we turn the final page of this journey, let us carry forward the lessons and insights gleaned from the Moedim. May they continue to inspire and guide us, illuminating our paths as we navigate the complexities of modern life while holding fast to the timeless traditions that define and enrich the Jewish experience.

Chapter 15.

The conclusion to the Moedim from a Messianic Jewish perspective.

We have also arrived at the end of our **Messianic Jewish** exploration of the Moedim, which has taken us through the rich tapestry of Jewish festivals and holy days through the lens of Messianic Judaism. This journey has deepened our understanding of these ancient observances and illuminated their enduring significance and, above all else, how they find their fulfilment in the Messiah, Yeshua.

Throughout this exploration, we have recognised the moedim as more than mere historical commemorations or cultural practices. They are divinely appointed times, intricately woven into the fabric of Jewish life, each with a unique purpose and message. From the weekly Shabbat, a time of rest and reflection, to the solemn introspection of Yom Kippur, these festivals collectively represent a spiritual roadmap, guiding us through the seasons of individual and communal life.

In examining Pesach, we revisited the story of Israel's deliverance from Egypt, seeing it not only as a historical event but as a prophetic picture of redemption. The sacrificial lamb, unleavened bread, and the offering of the first fruit have taken on new meanings in the light of Yeshua's life, death, and resurrection. As the Lamb of God, Yeshua embodies the ultimate deliverance from the bondage of sin, offering us a path to spiritual freedom.

Shavuot traditionally marks the giving of the Torah at Mount Sinai. For Messianic Jews, this festival also celebrates the outpouring of the Holy Spirit, as described in the New Testament. This event symbolises the new covenant, where the Torah is written on our hearts, empowering us to live out God's commandments with love and sincerity.

The High Holy Days – Yom Teruah and Yom Kippur – bring us into a season of reflection, repentance, and renewal. In the sounding of the shofar, there is a call to awaken from spiritual slumber. Yom Kippur, the Day of Atonement, holds a particular significance in the Messianic Jewish understanding, as it points to Yeshua as our High Priest, who makes atonement for our sins once and for all.

Sukkot, or the Feast of Tabernacles, invites us to dwell in temporary shelters, reminding us of the Israelites' wilderness journey and God's faithful provision. In Messianic thought, this festival also anticipates the future kingdom, when Yeshua will reign, and God's presence will dwell among His people in a renewed world.

As we have journeyed through these moedim, we have seen how they are commemorations of past events and prophetic signposts pointing to the Messiah and the redemption he brings. They remind us of God's faithfulness throughout history and His ongoing work. Each festival, with its unique rituals and traditions, invites us into a deeper relationship with God, encouraging us to reflect on His goodness, repent of our shortcomings, and rejoice in His salvation.

Moreover, this journey has highlighted the interconnectedness of Jewish and Messianic faith traditions. For Messianic Jews, the moedim are a bridge that connects the Old and New Testaments, revealing the continuity of God's plan for humanity. They offer a unique perspective that enriches Messianic understandings of the Bible and God's redemptive narrative.

In embracing the moedim, Messianic Jews find a connection to their Jewish heritage and a deeper understanding of their faith in Yeshua. These holy days are a constant reminder of God's promises, His covenant with Israel, and our future hope in the Messiah. They challenge believers to live out their faith authentically and wholeheartedly, rooted in the rich soil of Scripture and tradition.

As we close this book, we are invited to continue our cyclical journey, exploring the depths of these ancient truths and their relevance for our daily lives. The moedim are not just historical footnotes or religious obligations; they are vibrant, living celebrations that offer insight, inspiration, and hope. They beckon us to enter the rhythm of God's calendar, align our lives with His purposes, and anticipate His kingdom's coming.

In summary, "A Journey Through the Moedim" is more than a study of festivals; it is an invitation to a deeper, more integrated faith. It challenges us to see the Messiah in every aspect of our spiritual journey, to embrace our heritage, and to live in the light of God's redemptive plan. As we turn the final page, we are not at the end but at a new beginning, called to walk in the footsteps of the Messiah, keeping our hearts and minds open to the profound lessons of the Moedim and God's fantastic timetable for His plan of salvation.

A MESSIANIC RECAP OF THE SCRIPTURAL MOEDIM.

REMEMBERING (Past)	FESTIVAL	PROPHESYING (Future)
7th day of rest after Creation	Shabbat (Shabbat)	Messianic Era (Hebrew 4:9-11)
Redemption from slavery to Egypt through the blood of **A** lamb	Pesach (Passover) *Fulfilled by Yeshua on His death.*	Redemption from slavery to sin through the blood of **THE** Lamb
Leaven had to be removed from their lives	HaMatzot (Unleavened Bread) *Fulfilled by Yeshua on His burial.*	Sin has to be removed from our lives
The start for God's people of a new life,	Bikkurim (First Fruit) *Fulfilled by Yeshua on His resurrection.*	Messiah's resurrection as the first fruit of the righteous gives us new life

Giving of the Torah written on stone	Shavuot (Pentecost) **Fulfilled by the Holy Spirit**	Giving of the Holy Spirit who writes God's Torah on our hearts
A shofar (trumpet) call for God's people to judgement	Yom Teruah (Trumpets) **Still to be fulfilled**	For the Lord Himself will descend with the sound of the shofar (1 Thess 4:16)
A call to a day of confession and repentance	Yom Kippur (Day of Atonement) **Still to be fulfilled**	Judgement to all on Messiah's return to the earth
1. God tabernacled (lived) among His people. 2. Yeshua came to live among His people	Sukkot (Tabernacles) **Still to be fulfilled**	The Messiah will return to live and reign among His people.

Book 2
Celebrating Tradition Beyond the Torah: Non-Biblical Jewish Holidays Unveiled

1. Introduction — 130
2. An overview of the main events. — 135
3. Asarah B'Tevet / Fast of Tevet. — 138
4. Hannukah / Festival of Light — 142
5. Lag BaOmer - 33rd day of the Omer — 147
6. Purim / feast of lots — 150
7. Tzom Tammuz / Seventeenth of Tammuz — 155
8. Tisha B'Av / Seventeenth of Tammuz — 158
9. Tu Bishvat / New year for the trees — 161
10. Yom HaAliyah / Alyiah day — 167
11. Yom HaShoah / Holocaust Remembrance Day — 171
12. Yom Ha'atzmaut / Israel Independence Day — 176
13. Yom Hazikaron / Memorial Day — 181
14. Yom Yerushalayim / Yerushalayim Day — 185
15. What have we learned? — 189
16. This is only the beginning. — 192

Book Two.

Chapter 1.

Introduction

The Jewish community celebrates various holidays with deep cultural and historical significance throughout the year. Not directly ordained in the Torah, these holidays stem from various periods and events in Jewish history. Each of these observances plays a role in the cultural and spiritual life of the Jewish people, offering a rich tapestry of traditions, stories, and customs.

The origins of these holidays are diverse, with some tracing back to the ancient times of Jewish history, while others are of more recent origin. They commemorate significant historical events, celebrate Jewish resilience and survival, and often reflect the continuous struggle and triumphs of the Jewish people throughout history. These days of remembrance and celebration are a window into the past and a bridge connecting the modern Jewish community to its rich heritage.

One of the most striking aspects of these holidays is their ability to blend solemnity with joy. Some of these days commemorate events that were pivotal in shaping the Jewish identity and experience. They often begin with reflective practices, remembering the struggles and sacrifices of their ancestors.

This remembrance serves as a reminder of the resilience and endurance of the Jewish spirit through various trials and tribulations. Following these moments of reflection, the mood shifts to celebration and joy, emphasising the triumphs and resilience over adversity. This duality of solemnity and celebration is a core characteristic of these holidays, embodying the Jewish spirit's depth and complexity.

The customs and traditions associated with these holidays are as varied as their origins. Many involve special prayers and readings that are unique to the occasion. These readings often recount the historical events being commemorated, serving to educate and remind the younger generations of their heritage. These holidays typically feature unique culinary traditions, with special foods prepared and enjoyed. These dishes are often symbolic, representing various aspects of the holiday's history and significance.

Another important aspect of these holidays is the emphasis on community and family. These are times when families gather together, often welcoming friends and community members into their homes. There's a profound sense of unity and belonging when individuals unite to honor traditions inherited from ancestors. These occasions serve as opportunities for celebration and reinforcing connections within the community, bridging generational gaps.

These holidays also serve as an opportunity for introspection and personal growth. Many include customs encouraging individuals to reflect on their actions, relationships with others, and their place in the world. This reflective aspect is essential to the holiday experience, fostering personal and spiritual growth within the community.

In addition to their religious and cultural significance, these holidays also have a social impact. They often involve acts of charity and kindness, emphasising the Jewish values of helping those in need and contributing to the betterment of society. This aspect of the holidays strengthens the sense of responsibility and compassion within the Jewish community and towards the broader society.

Education plays a crucial role in these holidays. In addition to the historical narratives, many of these days are used as an opportunity to teach broader themes such as freedom, justice, and perseverance against adversity. These themes are central to the Jewish experience and universal, resonating with people of all backgrounds.

In conclusion, many of the non-Biblical Jewish holidays offer a rich and multifaceted experience, blending history, tradition, and spirituality. These holidays, each with unique significance and customs, contribute to the tapestry of Jewish life. They are a testament to the enduring spirit of the Jewish people, their resilience in the face of adversity, and their commitment to preserving their rich heritage. As such, they serve not only as a link to the past but also as a guiding light for the future, ensuring that the lessons and values of these holidays continue to inspire and guide the Jewish community for generations to come.

This book is intended to serve as a foundational reference guide, specifically highlighting a selection of the most widely recognised and commonly celebrated non-Scriptural events within contemporary Judaism.

While this compilation offers a diverse array of significant occasions, it's essential to understand that it doesn't aim to provide an exhaustive catalogue of all Jewish non-Scriptural celebrations, nor does this work prioritise events based on their importance or significance within the Jewish faith. This approach is intended to enhance understanding and appreciation of Jewish cultural and religious practices without implying a hierarchy of importance.

Messianic Jews generally adhere to all the festivals commanded in Scripture but recognise that lessons can be drawn from various non-scriptural festivals. However, it's important to note that not all these are universally celebrated within the Messianic Jewish community.

Among the non-scriptural festivals, Hanukkah and Purim are the most widely accepted and celebrated by Messianic Jewish believers. These are observed in ways that closely align with traditional Jewish customs.

May your journey into these short studies of some of the more commonly celebrated non-scriptural Jewish festivals be filled with enlightening discoveries and profound insights, and may this exploration deepen your understanding of cultural traditions, bringing you closer to the rich tapestry of Jewish history and communal life.

Chapter 2.

An overview.

- **Asarah B'Tevet:** This is a minor Jewish fast day commemorating the siege of Yerushalayim by Nebuchadnezzar II of Babylon, which led to the destruction of the First Temple.

- **Hanukkah:** Also known as the Festival of Lights, Hanukkah is an eight-day Jewish holiday commemorating the rededication of the Second Temple in Yerushalayim. It is marked by the lighting of the hanukkiah, traditional foods, games, and gifts.

- **Lag BaOmer:** This is a festive day on the Jewish calendar, celebrated with outings, bonfires, parades, and other joyous events. It marks the 33rd day of the Counting of the Omer, a period between Passover and Shavuot.

- **Purim:** A joyous Jewish holiday that commemorates the saving of the Jewish people from Haman, a Persian Empire official who planned to kill all the Jews, as recounted in the Book of Esther. It's celebrated with costume-wearing, feasting, and often with the giving of gifts.

- **Tzom Tammuz:** A fast day that marks the beginning of a three-week mourning period leading up to Tisha B'Av. It commemorates the breach of Yerushalayim's walls before the Second Temple's destruction.

- **Tisha B'Av:** A day of mourning and fasting in Judaism, commemorating the destruction of the First and Second Temples in Yerushalayim. It's considered the saddest day in the Jewish calendar.

- **Tu Bishvat:** Known as the "New Year for Trees", this is a Jewish holiday that occurs on the 15th day of Shevat. It is celebrated as an ecological awareness day, and trees are often planted in celebration.

- **Yom HaAliyah:** A relatively new holiday, it acknowledges Aliyah, the immigration of Jews from the diaspora to the Land of Israel. It's observed in Israel on the 10th of Nisan, marking the Israelites' entry into the Land of Israel led by Joshua, and on the 7th of Cheshvan in the civil calendar for broader public and school observance, as the former often coincides with Pesach.

- **Yom HaShoah:** Also known as Holocaust Remembrance Day, this day is observed as a day of commemoration for the approximately six million Jews, including about two million children and babies, who perished in the Holocaust as a result of the actions carried out by Nazi Germany.

- **Yom Ha'atzmaut:** Israeli Independence Day celebrates the establishment of the State of Israel in 1948.

- **Yom Hazikaron:** Israel's Memorial Day, commemorated on the day preceding Yom Ha'atzmaut. It honours Israeli military personnel who lost their lives in the struggle for the establishment of the State of Israel and in subsequent battles.

- **Yom Yerushalayim:** Yerushalayim Day commemorates the reunification of Yerushalayim and the establishment of Israeli control over the Old City in June 1967 after the Six-Day War.

Chapter 3.

Asarah B'Tevet / Fast of Tevet

Asarah B'Tevet, the Tenth of Tevet, is a significant day in the Jewish calendar marked by fasting and solemn reflection. It is a day when the Jewish community commemorates the siege of Yerushalayim and the events that ultimately led to the destruction of the First Temple. This day holds great historical and religious significance, offering a valuable opportunity for Jews to remember their past and draw vital lessons for the present and the future.

The origins of Asarah B'Tevet trace back to the biblical era, specifically to the time of the Babylonian exile. In 587 BCE, the Babylonian king Nebuchadnezzar laid siege to Yerushalayim, initiating a tragic chapter in Jewish history. This siege marked the beginning of a series of events that would culminate in the destruction of the First Temple, the exile of the Jewish people to Babylon, and the loss of Jewish sovereignty in their homeland.

The Tenth of Tevet is observed on the tenth day of the Jewish month of Tevet, which usually falls in December or early January in the Gregorian calendar. It is a day of fasting from dawn until nightfall, during which observant Jews abstain from eating or drinking. The fast begins at daybreak and continues until the stars appear in the evening sky. Unlike other Jewish fasts, observed with additional prayers and rituals, Asarah B'Tevet primarily involves fasting to remember and mourn past events.

The Tenth of Tevet serves as a solemn reminder of the destruction of the First Temple and the exile of the Jewish people. During the Babylonian siege, Yerushalayim faced unimaginable suffering, including a severe shortage of food and resources. The fast on Asarah B'Tevet allows Jews to empathise with their ancestors' suffering and to reflect on the consequences of their actions.

In addition to fasting, many Jews attend synagogue services on Asarah B'Tevet. Special prayers and readings from the Hebrew Bible are recited to remember past events and seek guidance for the future. The Torah portion often read on this day includes the prophecy of Ezekiel, who lived during the Babylonian exile and offered hope and encouragement to his fellow exiles.

The prophecy of Ezekiel is found in Ezekiel 24:1-14. In this prophecy, Ezekiel relays the word of God, informing him that on that very day, the siege against Yerushalayim will begin. The passage uses the metaphor of a cooking pot to describe the siege and the forthcoming calamity. It emphasises the severity of the impending destruction and the punishment that the people of Yerushalayim will face due to their iniquities. This chapter directly relates to the events that the day commemorates.

Asarah B'Tevet also carries a broader message that transcends its historical context. It teaches crucial lessons about the consequences of our actions, the value of unity, and the need for self-reflection.

One of the central lessons of Asarah B'Tevet is the recognition that actions have consequences. The siege of Yerushalayim and the subsequent destruction of the First Temple were not arbitrary events; they were the result of political and moral choices made by the Jewish people and their leaders. The fast serves as a reminder that our decisions and behaviours can have far-reaching effects, both individually and collectively. It encourages us to consider the consequences of our actions and strive for righteousness and justice in our lives.

Furthermore, Asarah B'Tevet underscores the importance of unity within the Jewish community. The events leading to the destruction of the First Temple were marked by internal strife and division among the Jewish people. The lack of unity weakened their ability to withstand external threats, ultimately contributing to their downfall. This lesson resonates today as a reminder of the value of unity and cooperation within any community, especially in times of adversity.

The day of fasting also provides an opportunity for self-reflection and introspection. It encourages individuals to assess their actions and attitudes and consider how they can contribute positively to their communities and the world. It is a day to ask oneself questions about personal responsibility, ethics, and values.

Moreover, Asarah B'Tevet serves as a call to remember and preserve Jewish history and heritage. By commemorating this day, Jews ensure that the memory of the First Temple, the Babylonian exile, and the enduring resilience of their people live on. It reinforces the importance of passing down these stories and lessons to future generations, ensuring that the mistakes of the past are not repeated.

In a broader context, Asarah B'Tevet invites individuals of all backgrounds to reflect on their histories and learn from the lessons of the past. It reminds us that history is not just a series of events but a repository of wisdom and insight that can guide our actions and decisions in the present and future.

In conclusion, Asarah B'Tevet is a day of fasting and commemoration that holds deep historical and spiritual significance for the Jewish community. It marks the beginning of the tragic events that led to the destruction of the First Temple and the Babylonian exile.

Beyond its historical context, Asarah B'Tevet offers valuable lessons about the consequences of our actions, the importance of unity, and the need for self-reflection. It encourages individuals to remember and preserve their history and heritage and to draw inspiration from the past to shape a more just and ethical future. As we fast on this day, we remember not only the suffering of our ancestors but also the enduring resilience and wisdom of the Jewish people.

'While history is irreversible, we can decide what of our past belongs in our future.'

Chapter 4.

Hanukkah.

The Festival of Lights and its Timeless Message

Hanukkah is a significant festival celebrated by millions of Jews worldwide. This holiday, often called the "Festival of Lights," holds significant historical and cultural significance within the Jewish community. Hanukkah celebrates faith, resilience, and the triumph of light over darkness.

In this chapter, we explore the origins of Hanukkah, the traditional ways it is celebrated, and the valuable lessons it imparts to people of all backgrounds.

Hanukkah has its roots in the events that transpired over 2,000 years ago in ancient Judea, which is now part of modern-day Israel. The story of Hanukkah revolves around the Maccabean Revolt, a historic struggle for religious freedom and Jewish identity against the oppressive Seleucid Empire.

Antiochus IV, also known as Antiochus Epiphanes, the Seleucid king, sought to Hellenize the Jewish people by enforcing Greek customs and religious practices. This included desecrating the Jewish temple in Yerushalayim, forbidding the practice of Judaism, and persecuting those who remained faithful to their traditions.

Two of the most infamous acts were the sacrificing of a pig on the Temple altar and placing an idol in the Temple, acts of blasphemy that deeply wounded Jewish religious sentiment.

The Maccabean Revolt against this was led by a group of Jewish warriors known as the Maccabees, or Hasmoneans, led by a priest, Judah Maccabee.

Despite being vastly outnumbered and outmatched, the Maccabees managed to reclaim the Holy Temple in Yerushalayim from the vastly numerically superior Seleucid forces in 164 BCE. Upon their victory, they embarked on a mission to purify and rededicate the temple, which involved rekindling the Menorah, the seven-branched candelabrum central to Jewish worship.

The most famous aspect of the Hanukkah story is the miraculous event that followed the temple's rededication. According to Jewish tradition, when the Maccabees sought to light the Menorah, they found only a tiny amount of oil, enough for one day. However, the Menorah remained alight for eight days until new, consecrated oil could be prepared. This divine miracle emphasises the significance of Hanukkah's eight-day duration.

It marks the origin of the 9-branch candelabrum, called the Hanukkiah, which is the primary symbol of Hanukkah, and is used to commemorate the oil miracle. Each night of Hanukkah, a new candle is lit, starting with the centre candle, known as the "shamash," or servant, used to light the others. This ritual reflects the increasing light and hope brought into the world during the festival's eight days.

In addition to lighting the Hanukkiah, other traditions and customs are associated with Hanukkah. Families often gather to play dreidel, a spinning top game with Hebrew letters on the sides of the spinner, symbolising the miracle of Hanukkah. Special foods, such as latkes (potato pancakes) and sufganiyot (jam-filled doughnuts), are prepared and enjoyed during the holiday. These foods are traditionally fried in oil as an additional reminder of the miraculous oil that burned in the temple.

Giving and receiving small gifts is another cherished Hanukkah tradition, with children sometimes receiving small presents each night of the festival. This custom reinforces the spirit of giving and the importance of family and community during this celebration.

As previously mentioned, the nightly lighting of the Hanukkiah is the centrepiece of Hanukkah celebrations. It is a moment of reflection and gratitude for the miracles of the past and a symbol of hope for the future.

The lighting traditionally takes place just after sunset, and blessings are recited, commemorating the miraculous events of Hanukkah. Families gather around the Hanukkiah, singing traditional songs and enjoying each other's company in the warm glow of the candles.

The tradition is to place the Hanukkiah in the window where the light can be clearly seen. The tradition of placing it in a window (or a place where others can see it) is to publicise the miracle of Hanukkah. This practice teaches the importance of sharing our stories and victories, inspiring others and strengthening community bonds.

Beyond the historical narrative and the rituals, Hanukkah imparts several valuable lessons that are universally relevant and can resonate with people of all backgrounds.

Hanukkah's story underscores the Jewish people's resilience

in the face of great oppression and adversity. It teaches us the importance of standing up for one's beliefs and enduring in the pursuit of justice and freedom. Hanukkah reminds us that even in the darkest times, the human spirit can triumph over adversity.

The miracle of the oil, a central aspect of Hanukkah, serves as a testament to the enduring power of faith and hope in the God of Israel. It teaches us that even when the odds seem insurmountable, a steadfast belief in the possibility of miracles can lead to unexpected outcomes.

Hanukkah highlights the importance of religious freedom and tolerance. It reminds us that every individual and community should have the right to practise their faith without fear of persecution or discrimination. This message resonates with people of most faiths and backgrounds, even those with no acknowledged faith, emphasising the need for mutual respect and understanding.

Hanukkah encourages families and communities to come together in celebration. It highlights the importance of spending quality time with loved ones, sharing traditions, and fostering a sense of unity and belonging.

The lighting of the Hanukkiah symbolises the triumph of light over darkness, both literally and metaphorically. It serves as a reminder that even in the darkest times, there is always a glimmer of hope and the potential for positive change.

In conclusion, Hanukkah, the Festival of Lights, is a celebration deeply rooted in Jewish history and tradition. It commemorates the triumph of faith, resilience, and the enduring power of hope in the face of adversity.

Beyond its specific cultural and religious significance, Hanukkah offers valuable lessons that can inspire and resonate with people of all backgrounds. It reminds us of the importance of standing up for our beliefs, the enduring power of faith, and the value of religious freedom, unity, and togetherness.

Hanukkah is a timeless source of inspiration and a beacon of light in a world often marked by challenges and darkness.

"A little light dispels a lot of darkness." – Rabbi Schneur Zalman of Liadi

"We light candles for the miracles, the salvations, and the wonders." - The Talmud, Shabbat 21b

Chapter 5.

Lag B'Omer - 33rd day of the counting of the Omer.

A Celebration of Unity and Resilience

Lag B'Omer, also known as the 33rd day of the Omer, is a significant Jewish holiday celebrated on the 18th day of the Hebrew month of Iyar.

This holiday holds a unique place in Jewish tradition, as it marks a break from the period of mourning that spans the first 32 days of the Omer, and it is a day of joy and celebration. To truly understand the significance of Lag B'Omer, it is essential to explore its origins, how it is generally celebrated, and the valuable lessons it imparts to those who observe it.

The origins of Lag B'Omer are deeply rooted in Jewish history and mysticism. The Omer is a seven-week period between Pesach and Shavuot, during which Jewish tradition dictates a period of semi-mourning to commemorate the deaths of Rabbi Akiva's 24,000 students who died from a plague.

Lag B'Omer, however, is a day of respite amid this mourning period. It is believed to be the day when the plague ceased, allowing Rabbi Akiva's students to survive.

The holiday also holds significance as it marks the yahrzeit, or anniversary of the passing, of Rabbi Shimon bar Yochai, a renowned sage and author of the Zohar, a fundamental work in Jewish mysticism known as Kabbalah. (For a brief explanation of Kabbalah, see the end of chapter 9).

According to Jewish tradition, Rabbi Shimon revealed deep mystical insights on his passing, making Lag B'Omer a day of spiritual elevation and enlightenment. Lag B'Omer is celebrated with various customs and traditions, creating a vibrant and joyful atmosphere.

One of the most well-known customs is the lighting of bonfires. Communities often come together to ignite large bonfires, symbolising the spiritual light and wisdom attributed to Rabbi Shimon. These bonfires also serve as a reminder of the light that emerged after the darkness of the plague that afflicted Rabbi Akiva's students.

Another common tradition is the custom of haircutting for young boys who have reached the age of three. This practice is tied to the legend that during the Omer period, Rabbi Akiva's students perished because they did not show each other enough respect. The respite provided by Lag B'Omer signifies a fresh start, and the first haircut represents a renewed commitment to unity and respect among the Jewish community.

Many Jews also visit the tomb of Rabbi Shimon bar Yochai in the northern Israeli town of Meron, where grand celebrations occur, including dancing, singing, and prayer. This pilgrimage to Rabbi Shimon's tomb is a testament to the enduring significance of his teachings and the belief in the spiritual blessings associated with Lag B'Omer.

Lag B'Omer imparts valuable lessons to those who celebrate it.

First and foremost, it teaches the importance of unity within the Jewish community. The tragic fate of Rabbi Akiva's students serves as a poignant reminder that internal strife and discord can have devastating consequences. Lag B'Omer symbolises the opportunity for reconciliation and the rebuilding of communal bonds.

Furthermore, the holiday encourages individuals to seek spiritual growth and enlightenment. Rabbi Shimon's teachings emphasise the pursuit of inner wisdom and connection with the Divine. Lag B'Omer serves as a reminder to reflect on one's spiritual journey and to strive for greater understanding and closeness to God.

In conclusion, Lag B'Omer is a unique and meaningful holiday in the Jewish calendar. Its origins in the aftermath of tragedy, the celebration of Rabbi Shimon's teachings, and the customs associated with the day all contribute to its rich significance.

Above all, Lag B'Omer teaches us the importance of unity, reconciliation, and spiritual growth. As Jews come together to celebrate this special day, they commemorate the past and look forward to a brighter and more harmonious future.

'Strength and growth come only through continuous effort and struggle.' - Rabbi Shimon bar Yochai

Chapter 6.

Purim.

A Celebration of Unity and Resilience

Purim is a joyous Jewish holiday that commemorates the miraculous deliverance of the Jewish people from the hands of a genocidal plot in ancient Persia. It is celebrated with great enthusiasm and devotion by Jewish communities worldwide. This chapter aims to provide a comprehensive understanding of Purim by exploring its origins, traditional customs, and the valuable lessons it imparts.

The origins of Purim are rooted in the biblical Book of Esther, known as the Megillah, which tells the story of Esther, a Jewish woman who becomes the Queen of Persia.

The narrative unfolds in the 5th century BCE when the Persian Empire extended over 127 provinces, including the land of Israel. King Ahasuerus (often identified as Xerxes I) ruled the empire then.

The story begins with King Ahasuerus holding a lavish banquet, during which he demands that his queen, Vashti, appear before his guests. Vashti refuses, leading to her dismissal. Subsequently, a new queen is sought, and Esther, a Jewish orphan raised by her cousin Mordecai, is chosen as the new queen. However, Esther conceals her Jewish identity, as advised by Mordecai, to protect herself from potential discrimination.

The story's main antagonist is Haman, a high-ranking Persian court official who harbours a deep-seated hatred for

Mordecai. Haman devises a wicked plan to annihilate all the Jews in the empire, using the casting of lots (purim) to determine the date for their extermination. The lot falls on the 13th day of Adar.

Mordecai learns of Haman's nefarious plot and urges Esther to intercede with the king to save their people. Despite the great danger, Esther courageously approaches the king, revealing her Jewish heritage and pleading for the salvation of her people. Ahasuerus, unaware of Haman's evil scheme, issues a counter-decree allowing the Jews to defend themselves against their attackers on the appointed day.

As the day of reckoning arrives, the Jews successfully thwart Haman's plan, leading to the execution of Haman himself and a resounding victory for the Jewish people.

To commemorate this miraculous turn of events, the holiday of Purim is established on the 14th day of Adar. Purim is a vibrant and spirited holiday celebrated with religious customs, festive activities, and community engagement. Here are some of the critical elements of how Purim is typically celebrated:

The central ritual of Purim is the public reading of the Book of Esther, also known as the Megillah. This reading is generally performed twice during Purim: once in the evening and again in the morning. Congregations gather in synagogues, and whenever the name of Haman is mentioned, it is customary to drown out his name with a loud noise, often using noisemakers called "graggers."

Purim is frequently referred to as the Jewish carnival. One of the most enjoyable aspects of the holiday is dressing up in costumes, similar to Halloween. This tradition is rooted in the idea that during the Purim story, Esther concealed her true identity, so Jews today "hide" their own identities with costumes. Dressing up in creative and elaborate outfits adds a fun and playful dimension to the holiday.

Another essential custom of Purim is the exchange of gifts known as "Mishloach Manot." Families and friends give each other baskets filled with various foods, snacks, and sweets. These gift baskets symbolise the importance of unity and friendship within the Jewish community.

On Purim, Jews are also encouraged to give to those in need through "Matanot L'Evyonim," which translates to "gifts for the poor." It is a way of ensuring that everyone can join in the celebration, regardless of their financial circumstances. This practice emphasises the value of compassion and charity.

Purim is a time for feasting and merrymaking. Families and friends come together to enjoy festive meals and traditional Purim foods, such as hamantaschen, a triangular-shaped pastry filled with various sweet fillings. These meals foster a sense of community and joy.

In some Jewish communities, particularly in Israel, Purim is marked with lively street parades known as "Adloyada." These parades feature colourful floats, music, and performances, adding to the festive atmosphere.

While Purim is a festive and joyful holiday, it also carries profound lessons and messages that resonate with people of all backgrounds. Here are some of the valuable lessons we can learn from Purim:

The story of Esther exemplifies the importance of courage

and standing up against injustice, even in the face of personal risk. Esther's bravery in approaching King Ahasuerus to plead for the lives of her people serves as a timeless example of moral fortitude.

Purim underscores the significance of unity within the Jewish community. Mordecai and Esther's collaboration, along with the collective efforts of the Jewish people, led to their salvation. The exchange of gifts (Mishloach Manot) and charitable acts (Matanot L'Evyonim) on Purim reinforce the idea of communal support and solidarity.

The casting of lots (purim) by Haman to determine the date of the Jewish extermination is a reminder of the unpredictability of fate. Purim teaches us that life can be full of unexpected twists, and we must be prepared to confront adversity with resilience and resourcefulness.

Purim celebrates the ultimate triumph of good over evil. Haman's sinister plot is thwarted, and justice prevails. This message of hope and the belief that righteousness will ultimately prevail resonates with people from diverse backgrounds.

The theme of concealment and revelation in the Purim story reminds us of the importance of authenticity and the power of revealing one's true self when necessary. Esther's initial concealment of her identity contrasts with her eventual revelation to the king, which played a pivotal role in saving her people.

Purim encourages a spirit of gratitude and joy. The holiday is a time to express gratitude for the Jewish people's deliverance and to find joy in the company of loved ones and the celebration of life's blessings.

In conclusion, Purim is a vibrant and meaningful Jewish holiday commemorating the miraculous events recounted in the Book of Esther. It celebrates courage, unity, and the triumph of good over evil. Through customs like reading the Megillah, wearing costumes, and giving gifts to the poor, Purim brings the Jewish community together in joyous festivities that carry valuable lessons for people of all backgrounds.

"It is a great mitzvah (commandment) to be happy always and to make every effort to determine a positive judgement on everyone." Rabbi Nachman of Breslov.

Chapter 7.

Tzom Tammuz - Seventeenth of Tammuz.

"Reflection and Remembrance"

Tzom Tammuz, or the Fast of Tammuz, is an annual Jewish fast day commemorating the breaching of Yerushalayim's walls before the destruction of the Second Temple. This significant event in Jewish history holds great religious, historical, and cultural importance. The fast occurs on the 17th day of the Hebrew month of Tammuz and marks the beginning of a three-week mourning period leading up to Tisha B'Av, commemorating the destruction of the First and Second Temples.

The origins of Tzom Tammuz are rooted in the turbulent history of the Jewish people. According to the Talmud, the fast commemorates not only the breach of Yerushalayim's walls by the Babylonians in 586 BCE and the Romans in 70 CE but also other calamities that befell the Jewish people on the same date. These include the shattering of Moses's first set of Tablets of the Law and the cessation of the daily offerings during the Roman siege of Yerushalayim.

The observance of Tzom Tammuz involves fasting from dawn until nightfall and refraining from eating or drinking. Unlike Yom Kippur or Tisha B'Av, Tzom Tammuz is considered a minor fast. Nonetheless, it is a day marked by solemnity and introspection.

Many Jews engage in additional prayer and Torah study, reflecting on the themes of loss, destruction, and the hope for redemption. Some communities hold special prayer services, including the recitation of Selichot (penitential prayers) and reading portions of the Book of Lamentations.

The fast expresses mourning over historical events and a time for personal and communal introspection. The destruction of the Temple is often interpreted as a consequence of moral and spiritual failings, such as baseless hatred and ethical corruption.

Tzom Tammuz, therefore, provides an opportunity for Jews to examine their actions and to strive for personal improvement and communal harmony. It is a time to consider how individuals and communities can contribute to a more just and compassionate society.

The lessons of Tzom Tammuz extend beyond the Jewish community. The themes of destruction and renewal, loss and hope, are universal. The fast day reminds us that even in the face of tragedy and despair, there is the potential for growth and rebuilding. It encourages reflection on the impermanence of physical structures and institutions and the enduring importance of spiritual and moral values.

Moreover, Tzom Tammuz offers a perspective on the significance of memory in shaping identity and values. By recalling past tragedies, the fast day underscores the importance of learning from history, acknowledging past mistakes, and working towards a better future. It is a call to remember the moments of destruction and the resilience and strength that have allowed communities to rebuild and thrive in the aftermath.

In summary, Tzom Tammuz is a day of fasting and reflection that holds deep significance in Jewish tradition. It commemorates historical events symbolic of loss and destruction and catalyses introspection, moral improvement, and communal harmony. The lessons of Tzom Tammuz resonate beyond the Jewish community, offering universal insights into the themes of memory, resilience, and the enduring power of hope.

As such, it is a day that invites all to consider how they can contribute to a more compassionate and just world.

Chapter 8.

Tisha B'Av - Ninth of Av.

A Joyous Celebration of Survival and Unity

Tisha B'Av, the ninth day of the Hebrew month of Av, stands as one of the most solemn dates on the Jewish calendar, embodying a day of mourning and fasting. Its origins trace back to ancient times, specifically to pivotal events that have indelibly marked the Jewish people's history with sorrow and devastation.

Over centuries, Tisha B'Av has evolved to commemorate multiple tragedies, becoming a day that encapsulates the enduring spirit of a community faced with repeated loss yet also highlights the resilience and hope that defines the Jewish faith and identity.

The initial association of Tisha B'Av with calamity begins with the Biblical narrative of the spies sent by Moses to scout the Land of Canaan. According to tradition, the negative report brought back by ten of the twelve spies and the subsequent despair and lack of faith shown by the Israelites led to God decreeing that the generation who witnessed the miraculous events of the Exodus would not enter the Promised Land. This event, occurring on the ninth of Av, set a precedent for the day as one of misfortune and divine judgment.

The most central events Tisha B'Av commemorates are the destruction of the First and Second Temples in Jerusalem, pivotal moments that reshaped Jewish history.

The First Temple, built by King Solomon, was destroyed

by the Babylonians in 586 BCE, leading to the exile of the Jewish people to Babylon.

Approximately 656 years later, the Second Temple met a similar fate at the hands of the Roman Empire in 70 CE, marking the start of a long diaspora.

These destructions are not merely historical events; they symbolise the loss of Jewish sovereignty, the beginning of the exile, and the profound spiritual grief over the loss of the central place of worship and divine presence.

Over time, Tisha B'Av has come to memorialise additional tragedies that have befallen the Jewish people on or around this date.

These include the 360-year expulsion of Jews from England in 1290, the expulsion from Spain in 1492, and numerous other pogroms, massacres, and periods of suffering throughout Jewish history.

The day has thus morphed into a collective memory of persecution and loss, serving as a historical ledger that records the recurring themes of exile and survival against the odds.

The observance of Tisha B'Av is marked by several unique traditions that reflect the day's mournful character. Fasting from sunset on the eve of Tisha B'Av until nightfall the following day is the most prominent practice, symbolising the sombre reflection and mourning.

Other customs include sitting on low stools or the floor, as is customary during periods of mourning, abstaining from wearing leather footwear and refraining from engaging in pleasurable activities such as bathing, music, and study of Torah, except for texts related to Tisha B'Av.

The recitation of Eicha (the Book of Lamentations) and Kinot (elegies) during the evening and morning services, respectively, further embody the themes of destruction, loss, and the yearning for redemption.

From Tisha B'Av, a profound lesson of resilience and faith emerges. It serves as a poignant reminder of the cyclical nature of history and the enduring spirit required to face adversity.

The day encourages reflection on the collective and personal challenges faced by individuals and communities, emphasising the importance of faith, the value of remembering the past, and the hope for future redemption.

Tisha B'Av is not only about mourning; it is also about the contemplation of the moral and spiritual lessons learned from these historical calamities and applying these lessons towards building a more hopeful, unified, and resilient future.

In this reflection and yearning, the essence of Tisha B'Av transcends the bounds of time, linking past, present, and future in a continuous thread of collective memory, identity, and hope.

Chapter 9.

Tu Bishvat - New Year for the Trees.

Celebrating the New Year for Trees and Embracing Environmental Stewardship

Tu Bishvat, also known as the "New Year of the Trees," is a Jewish holiday celebrating nature's awakening and the beginning of the agricultural cycle. It falls on the 15th day of the Hebrew month of Shevat, typically in late January or early February.

The holiday's name, "Tu Bishvat," is derived from its date in the Hebrew calendar: "Tu" stands for the Hebrew letters Tet and Vav, which together have the numerical value of 15, and "Bishvat" means "in Shevat."

The origins of Tu Bishvat are found in ancient Jewish law. In the Torah, specific laws govern the agricultural products of Israel. These laws include rules about tithing and setting aside a portion of the fruits for the priests and the poor, as well as the concept of "orlah," which forbids eating the fruit of a tree for its first three years.

The rabbis of the Talmudic era (200-500 CE) determined that Tu Bishvat should mark the new year for trees when the age of trees is calculated for these agricultural commandments.

Over the centuries, Tu Bishvat evolved from a legalistic observance into celebrating the natural world and our connection to it. The 16th-century Kabbalists created a new ritual for Tu Bishvat called the "Tu Bishvat Seder." (A very brief and simplistic overview of Kabbalah is given at the end of this chapter).

Inspired by the Pesach Seder, this ritual involves eating various fruits and nuts, drinking four cups of wine, and reciting blessings. The Kabbalists saw the fruits and trees as symbols of the divine and the Seder as a way to explore mystical concepts about nature and spirituality.

Today, Tu Bishvat is celebrated in various ways, reflecting its agricultural and mystical origins. In Israel, it is a day for ecological awareness and tree planting. Schoolchildren and families participate in tree-planting ceremonies, contributing to the reforestation efforts that have transformed much of Israel's 'desert' landscape.

This tradition has helped to cultivate a strong connection between the Jewish people and their historic homeland. Jews outside Israel celebrate Tu Bishvat by holding communal meals and enjoying fruits and nuts native to Israel.

The Seven Species in Deuteronomy are wheat, barley, grapes, figs, pomegranates, olives, and dates. In ancient Israel, these foods were so revered that they were offered during temple worship. Nowadays, they are celebrated during certain Jewish holidays and are often featured in Judaica and Jewish home decor.

Each species carries a unique spiritual significance according to Kabbalah, symbolising different attributes.

Wheat represents kindness, providing strength and positive energy, much like the mental strength kindness brings.

Barley symbolises strength and is known for its resilient

hull and ability to absorb water, paralleling our need to protect our souls and continually absorb the Torah.

Grapes, used in wine for rituals and celebrations, signify beauty and joy in life.

Figs, with their long ripening period and year-round availability, represent perseverance and the continuous pursuit of knowledge.

With their crown and gem-like seeds, pomegranates symbolise splendour and humility, reminding us to be humble yet let our true selves shine.

Olives, producing olive oil, stand for the foundation, illustrating the importance of adapting to life's bitterness and creating something valuable, like transforming bitter olives into delicious oil.

Lastly, dates, producing honey, are seen as royalty, representing the connection between attributes on the Kabbalistic Tree of Life and their longstanding cultural significance in Israel.

The Seven Species hold a special place in Judaism for their historical and cultural significance and spiritual symbolism. They are celebrated during harvest holidays like Sukkot, Shavuot, and Tu Bishvat. Eating these foods is a culinary experience and a way to connect with these profound meanings.

Tu Bishvat is also an opportunity for environmental education and activism. Synagogues, Jewish schools, and community organisations often organise events focused on ecological responsibility, such as recycling projects, lectures on sustainability, and discussions about Jewish environmental ethics. The holiday has become a type of Jewish Earth Day, inspiring people to reflect on their relationship with the environment and their responsibility to care for the earth.

Tu Bishvat offers several valuable lessons that extend beyond the Jewish community. It teaches us the importance of environmental stewardship. In an age where concerns about climate change and ecological degradation are paramount, Tu Bishvat reminds us that caring for the earth is not just a contemporary issue but a timeless moral imperative.

This holiday encourages us to appreciate the natural world and to take active steps to preserve and enhance it. By planting trees and engaging in environmentally friendly practices, we honour the traditions of the past and invest in a sustainable future.

Tu Bishvat underscores the concept of interconnectedness. Just as a tree's roots are interconnected with the soil, water, and air around it, so are we interconnected with our environment and each other. This holiday invites us to reflect on how our actions impact the world and strive for harmony and balance in our interactions with nature and fellow human beings.

Moreover, Tu Bishvat offers a perspective on time and patience. Like a tree that takes years to grow and bear fruit, many of the most important aspects of life require time and nurturing. The holiday teaches us the value of long-term thinking and the importance of nurturing growth and development, whether in nature, our personal lives, or our communities.

In addition, Tu Bishvat provides a platform for spiritual reflection. The Kabbalistic traditions associated with the holiday encourage us to look beyond the surface of things and to find deeper meanings and connections. The fruits and trees become metaphors for spiritual concepts, inviting us to contemplate our place in the universe and our relationship with the divine.

Tu Bishvat is a celebration of diversity and renewal. Just as a forest comprises various trees, each contributing to the ecosystem uniquely, our world is enriched by the diversity of cultures, ideas, and perspectives. The holiday, occurring in the dead of winter but signalling the coming of spring, reminds us that even in the darkest times, there is the promise of renewal and growth.

In conclusion, Tu Bishvat is much more than simply commemorating trees and agriculture. It is a complex and diverse holiday that speaks to our environmental responsibilities, interconnectedness, the importance of patience and long-term thinking, spiritual journey, and the celebration of diversity and renewal. Observing Tu Bishvat and reflecting on its lessons can deepen our appreciation of the natural world, strengthen our commitment to its preservation, and enhance our understanding of our place within it.

"When God created the first human beings, God led them around the Garden of Eden and said: 'Look at my works! See how beautiful they are — how excellent! For your sake I created them all. See to it that you do not spoil and destroy My world; for if you do, there will be no one else to repair it.'"
Midrash Kohelet Rabbah 7:13:

(Kabbalah is a mystical part of Judaism that started in the late 12th century. It's about trying to understand God and the universe better. It uses special ideas and practices, like the Tree of Life, to explore deep topics. A main part of Kabbalah is the "Sefirot," ten attributes that show how God works in the world. These Sefirot are like channels for God's energy and are arranged in the Tree of Life pattern.

The ten Sefirot are Keter (Crown), Chokhmah (Wisdom), Binah (Understanding), Chesed (Kindness), Gevurah (Severity), Tiferet (Beauty), Netzach (Eternity), Hod (Glory), Yesod (Foundation), and Malkuth (Kingdom).

Each represents different aspects of the divine and aims to help people understand spirituality.

Kabbalah is important in traditional Judaism, especially among Hasidic and Orthodox groups. It's used to try to understand God and the universe better and is part of their religious practices.

Messianic Judaism has different views on Kabbalah. Some Messianic Jews include some Kabbalistic ideas in their faith, while others don't think it fits their beliefs about the Messiah and the New Testament. How much Kabbalah influences Messianic Judaism depends on the person or group).

Chapter 10.

Yom HaAliyah - Aliyah Day.

Ascend to the Promised Land.

Yom HaAliyah, or Aliyah Day, is celebrated in Israel on the 10th of the Hebrew month of Nisan in the Jewish religious calendar. This date corresponds to the entry of the Israelites into the Land of Israel, as led by Joshua, according to the Hebrew Bible.

Yom HaAliyah is also observed in the civil Israeli calendar on the 7th of the Hebrew month of Cheshvan. This allows the holiday to be marked in schools and the public sphere at a more accessible time, as the 10th of Nisan typically falls during Passover.

The day acknowledges the immigration of Jews from the diaspora to the land of Israel and honours the ongoing contributions of immigrants to Israeli society. This day serves as a testament to the fulfilment of the Zionist dream and the integral role of Jewish immigration in the development and prosperity of the State of Israel.

The concept of Aliyah has deep roots in Jewish history and theology, stretching back to biblical times. The term "Aliyah" itself means "ascent" or "going up," reflecting the spiritual and moral elevation associated with moving to the Holy Land. This movement has been a central theme in Jewish life for millennia, often seen as a return to the ancestral homeland after centuries of exile. Throughout Jewish history, there have been several waves of Aliyah, each with unique circumstances and impact.

The modern history of Aliyah begins in the late 19th century with the rise of the Zionist movement, which sought to re-establish a Jewish homeland in Palestine. This period saw the First Aliyah (1882-1903), primarily from Eastern Europe and Yemen, where Jews faced persecution and sought refuge and a new life in their ancestral land. The subsequent waves of Aliyah, particularly the Second (1904-1914) and the Third (1919-1923), continued to build the foundations of what would become the State of Israel.

The establishment of Israel in 1948 marked a significant turning point. The new state enacted the Law of Return in 1950, granting every Jew the right to immigrate to Israel and obtain citizenship. This law catalyzed mass immigration from post-Holocaust Europe, Middle Eastern, and North African countries, dramatically reshaping the demographic and cultural landscape of Israel. The 1990s saw a large influx of immigrants from the former Soviet Union, further enriching Israeli society with diverse cultures and talents.

Yom HaAliyah was officially established as a national holiday in 2016, following a grassroots campaign by Jewish immigrants. The date, the tenth of Nisan, was chosen for its biblical significance; it is believed to be the day Joshua led the Israelites across the Jordan River into the Land of Israel. This date symbolises the link between the ancient biblical Aliyah and modern immigration to Israel.

Celebrations of Yom HaAliyah vary but often include ceremonies, educational events, and community gatherings. Schools across Israel engage in special programs and activities that educate students about the history and significance of Aliyah and the diverse backgrounds of immigrants who have helped shape the nation. In these educational settings, personal stories of immigrants are shared, highlighting their journeys and contributions to Israeli society.

Ceremonies and events are also held by various government institutions and organisations, often featuring speeches by public figures, cultural performances, and recognition of notable immigrants who have made significant contributions in multiple fields. These events serve not only to honour those who have made Aliyah but also to strengthen the bonds between native Israelis and immigrant communities.

Yom HaAliyah is more than just a celebration of past and present immigration; it's also a day to reflect on the ongoing challenges and opportunities of integrating diverse populations into a cohesive society.

Israel's unique melting pot of cultures, languages, and traditions, largely a result of decades of Aliyah, poses both challenges and opportunities in areas like education, employment, and social cohesion. The holiday serves as a reminder of the importance of embracing diversity and fostering a sense of unity and belonging among all citizens.

In addition to official events, Yom HaAliyah is celebrated informally within communities and families. Many use this day to share their own immigration stories, pass down family histories, and engage in discussions about their cultural heritage. For many, it's a day of personal reflection, recalling the struggles and triumphs of making a new life in Israel.

Another aspect of Yom HaAliyah is its global reach. Jewish

communities worldwide, particularly those with strong connections to Israel, often hold their celebrations. These events bridge the diaspora and Israel, reinforcing the global Jewish community's connection to the land and its people.

The significance of Yom HaAliyah extends beyond the Jewish and Israeli communities. It's a day that highlights the broader themes of migration, cultural integration, and the pursuit of a homeland, resonating with people and communities worldwide who have experienced similar journeys. It serves as a reminder of the universal aspirations for safety, freedom, and a better life that motivate people to leave their homes and seek new opportunities elsewhere.

In conclusion, Yom HaAliyah is a multifaceted holiday that celebrates the historical and ongoing journey of Jewish immigration to Israel. It's a day that honours the courage, determination, and contributions of immigrants who have played a crucial role in building and shaping the State of Israel.

Through various ceremonies, educational events, and personal reflections, Yom HaAliyah serves as a powerful reminder of the enduring bond between the Jewish people and their ancestral homeland, as well as the broader themes of migration and cultural integration relevant to societies worldwide.

Chapter 11.

Yom HaShoah - Holocaust Remembrance Day,

Echoes of Memory: Reflecting on Resilience and Remembrance

Yom HaShoah, also known as Holocaust Remembrance Day, is a day set aside to remember and honour the six million Jews who were murdered during the Holocaust, as well as the heroism of Jewish resistance during that period.

The Holocaust, one of the darkest chapters in human history, was the systematic, state-sponsored persecution and destruction of Jews by Nazi Germany and its collaborators between 1933 and 1945. Jews were the primary victims - six million were murdered; Roma (Gypsies), disabled individuals, Polish and Soviet civilians, homosexuals, Jehovah's Witnesses, and political dissidents were also persecuted and killed.

The term "genocide" was coined by Raphael Lemkin, a Polish-Jewish lawyer, in 1944. Lemkin created the term by combining the Greek word "genos," meaning race or tribe, with the Latin word "cide," meaning killing. His motivation for devising the term was to describe the systematic and deliberate extermination of a national, racial, or cultural group, particularly in reference to the Holocaust during World War II.

Lemkin's work, including the coining of the term "genocide," was instrumental in the establishment of the United Nations Convention on the Prevention and Punishment of the Crime of Genocide in 1948. This convention provided an international legal definition of genocide and set the legal framework for preventing and punishing such acts.

The commemoration of Yom HaShoah is a relatively recent phenomenon, reflecting the complex process of coming to terms with the Holocaust. The full magnitude and implications of the Nazi genocide took years to comprehend, and it was only over time that Yom HaShoah came to be widely recognised as a day of remembrance.

The origin of Yom HaShoah lies in the early post-war years. In 1951, the Israeli Parliament (Knesset) passed a law establishing a Holocaust and Ghetto Uprising Remembrance Day to be celebrated annually.

The chosen date, the 27th of Nisan in the Hebrew calendar, falls in April or May in the Gregorian calendar and was selected to coincide with the Warsaw Ghetto Uprising of 1943, one of the most significant acts of Jewish resistance during the Holocaust. This date intentionally falls after Passover, a festival of liberation, and before Israel's Independence Day, linking the memory of the Holocaust with the rebirth of the Jewish state.

Yom HaShoah is marked by solemn ceremonies and educational events that aim to remember the victims and teach the lessons of the Holocaust.

In Israel, the day is a national memorial day, beginning with a state ceremony at Yad Vashem, the World Holocaust Remembrance Center in Yerushalayim. At 10 a.m., a two-minute siren sounds throughout the country, during which Israelis stop all activity; public transport stops and cars stop while people exit their vehicles and join the nation as they stand in silence, honouring the victims. This moment of silence creates a powerful, unified experience of collective memory and reflection.

The observance of Yom HaShoah extends beyond Israel. Jewish communities around the world hold commemorative ceremonies, often including the recitation of names of Holocaust victims, memorial prayers, and the lighting of candles.

Educational programs also feature survivor testimonies, discussions, and exhibitions. These events aim to educate the public about the Holocaust, promote awareness, and encourage reflection on its moral and historical lessons.

The commemoration of Yom HaShoah also serves as an opportunity to confront and reject Holocaust denial and distortion. Denial and distortion of the Holocaust are forms of anti-Semitism, seeking to minimise or negate the suffering and murder of millions.

By remembering and teaching about the Holocaust, Yom HaShoah helps to counteract these dangerous falsehoods and ensure that the truth of what happened is preserved for future generations.

In recent years, Yom HaShoah has taken on additional significance as the number of Holocaust survivors diminishes. The firsthand accounts of survivors have been an essential part of Holocaust education and remembrance. As these voices fade, the responsibility to bear witness and educate about the Holocaust falls increasingly on younger generations. This transition poses challenges for Holocaust remembrance but offers new opportunities for engagement and learning.

The lessons of the Holocaust extend beyond the Jewish community and have universal implications. Yom HaShoah is an occasion to reflect on the dangers of unchecked hatred, racism, and totalitarianism.

It is a reminder of the importance of defending democratic values, human rights, and the dignity of every individual. The Holocaust teaches us that indifference and inaction can lead to unimaginable atrocities. Yom HaShoah thus calls on all people to stand against bigotry and injustice in all its forms.

In conclusion, Yom HaShoah, a day of remembrance for the victims of the Holocaust, carries profound significance. It's to mourn the loss of six million Jews and to honour their memory through education, reflection, and a commitment to preventing such tragedies in the future.

This day serves as a powerful reminder of the horrors that can occur when hatred and bigotry are allowed to flourish and the importance of standing up against such forces.

In a broader sense, Yom HaShoah transcends its specific historical context. It embodies the universal lessons of the Holocaust about the dangers of silence in the face of evil, the necessity of remembering the past, and the responsibility to protect the dignity and rights of all people.

The commemoration of Yom HaShoah is an act of remembrance and a call to action. It urges individuals and societies to confront hatred, promote human rights, and build a world where such atrocities are unthinkable. In this way, Yom HaShoah resonates with people of all backgrounds, serving as a beacon of hope and a reminder of the enduring human spirit in the face of the darkest times.

Through its observance, we remember the victims and honour their legacy by committing ourselves to building a better, more tolerant, and just world. The memory of the Holocaust and the observance of Yom HaShoah thus remain vital to our collective consciousness, compelling us to look back in sorrow but also forward with a determined hope for a brighter future.

"I swore never to be silent whenever and wherever human beings endure suffering and humiliation. We must always take sides. Neutrality helps the oppressor, never the victim. Silence encourages the tormentor, never the tormented." –

Elie Wiesel

Chapter 12.

Yom Ha'atzmaut - Israel Independence Day.

A Celebration of Renewal and Resilience.

Yom Ha'atzmaut, or Israel Independence Day, is a national holiday in Israel commemorating the declaration of Israel's independence in 1948. It is a day of great significance for the Jewish people and Israel, symbolising the realisation of the long-held dream of returning to their ancient homeland.

The holiday falls on the 5th day of the Hebrew month of Iyar, which usually corresponds to late April or early May in the Gregorian calendar. This date was selected to align with the Gregorian calendar date of the declaration, May 14, 1948.

The roots of Yom Ha'atzmaut trace back to the late 19th century, with the rise of Zionism, a nationalist movement among Jews to establish a modern Jewish state in the land of Israel, their ancestral homeland.

This movement gained momentum in the early 20th century, particularly after the Balfour Declaration of 1917, in which the British government expressed support for establishing a "national home for the Jewish people" in Palestine, then a British mandate.

The Holocaust during World War II, which saw the genocide of six million Jews, further intensified the urgency and desire for a Jewish state. Following the war, the United Nations approved a partition plan for Palestine in 1947, proposing the creation of separate Jewish and Arab states (known today as the two-state solution). This proposal was accepted by the Jews but rejected outright by all the Arab nations.

Despite opposition and conflict with neighbouring Arab states, David Ben-Gurion, the head of the Jewish Agency and the first Prime Minister of Israel, proclaimed the establishment of the State of Israel on May 14, 1948, in a ceremony in Tel Aviv.

This event was met with jubilation among Jews in the former British mandate of Palestine and around the world, but also marked the beginning of the 1948 Arab-Israeli War, as five large and well-armed neighbouring Arab states, Egypt, Iraq, Jordan, Lebanon, and Syria, attacked the fledgling nation.

The war resulted in significant territorial gains for Israel and the displacement of a large number of Arabs, a point of contention that remains central to the Israeli-Palestinian conflict, as they were listed as refugees, a status which has, uniquely, been handed down through subsequent generations.

Interestingly, an equal number of Jews were displaced from Arab countries. However, they were taken in by Israel rather than being left as refugees.

Yom Ha'atzmaut is celebrated with various ceremonies and events throughout Israel. The day begins with the official state ceremony at Mount Herzl, Yerushalayim, which includes lighting twelve torches, symbolising the Twelve Tribes of Israel. This is followed by the Israel Prize ceremony, where individuals and groups are honoured for their contributions to Israeli culture, science, and society.

Throughout the country, people celebrate with outdoor concerts, street parties, and barbecues (mangal in Hebrew). Israeli flags are prominently displayed, and many people wear blue and white, the colours of the Israeli flag. In addition to these festivities, the Israel Defense Forces (IDF) holds a military parade and air show, showcasing the country's military strength and technological advancements.

Cultural events, such as dance performances, music concerts, and museum exhibitions, also mark Yom Ha'atzmaut. Schools and community centres organise programs and activities for children, often focusing on the history and achievements of Israel.

This day is a time for Israelis to reflect on their national identity and the journey that led to the establishment of their state. It is a celebration of the realisation of a dream that dates back thousands of years – the return of the Jewish people to their ancestral homeland.

The significance of Yom Ha'atzmaut extends beyond the borders of Israel. Jewish communities worldwide celebrate this day, often organising events and activities in synagogues, schools, and community centres.

These celebrations typically include singing Israeli songs, dancing to traditional Israeli music, and enjoying Israeli cuisine. For many Jews in the diaspora, Yom Ha'atzmaut serves as a connection to their heritage and a celebration of Jewish unity and resilience.

The day before Yom Ha'atzmaut is Yom Hazikaron, Israel's Memorial Day for fallen soldiers and victims of terrorism, which is covered in more detail in the next chapter.

The juxtaposition of these two days is intentional and deeply symbolic. It underscores the sacrifices made to establish and maintain the State of Israel and serves as a reminder that independence was not achieved without cost. This transition from sorrow to joy is a unique aspect of Israeli culture and reflects the nation's ability to find hope and celebration amidst adversity.

Yom Ha'atzmaut has evolved over the years. Initially, it was a solemn day of reflection and gratitude, but it has become more festive and celebratory. This evolution reflects the changing nature of Israeli society and its growing confidence and prosperity. Today, Yom Ha'atzmaut is a day of national pride, celebrating Israel's achievements in various fields, including technology, medicine, and the arts.

However, Yom Ha'atzmaut is not without controversy. For Palestinians and some in the Arab world, the day is remembered as the Nakba, or "catastrophe," marking the displacement and loss that accompanied the establishment of Israel. This perspective is a reminder of the ongoing conflict and the region's complex history. Efforts to reconcile these narratives and find a path to peace continue to be challenging.

In conclusion, Yom Ha'atzmaut is a day of great importance for Israel and the Jewish people worldwide. It commemorates the historic declaration of independence and the realisation of a long-held dream. The celebrations reflect the Israeli people's joy, pride, and resilience while acknowledging the sacrifices and challenges that have shaped the nation's history.

As Israel continues to evolve, Yom Ha'atzmaut remains a symbol of hope, determination, and the enduring spirit of a people who have overcome tremendous adversity to build a vibrant and thriving nation.

David Ben-Gurion, the first Prime Minister of Israel, famously declared on May 14, 1948: "The State of Israel has arisen, and the dream of generations has been fulfilled."

Golda Meir, another Prime Minister of Israel, once said: "Independence is never given to a people; it has to be earned; and, once earned, must be defended."

Chapter 13.

Yom Hazikaron - Memorial Day.

Echoes of Remembrance: Israel's Solemn Day of Reflection.

Yom Hazikaron, or Israel's Memorial Day, is a day of profound significance, deeply ingrained in the Israeli psyche and national identity. It's a day set aside to remember and honour the soldiers who have fallen in defence of the State of Israel, as well as the civilian victims of terrorism.

Unlike many other countries where memorial days often include festive parades or celebratory events, Yom Hazikaron in Israel is marked by solemnity and reflection, a testament to the unique character of this day and the central place it holds in Israeli society.

The origins of Yom Hazikaron can be traced back to the early years of Israel's statehood. Established in 1951, four years after the end of the 1948 Arab-Israeli War, the day was initially set for the 4th of Iyar, the day preceding Israel's Independence Day.

This date was chosen to symbolically link the memory of sacrifice to the joy of independence, emphasising the price paid for the establishment and survival of the Jewish state. This juxtaposition of sorrow and celebration creates a powerful emotional transition from mourning to joy, from Yom Hazikaron to Yom Ha'atzmaut, Israel's Independence Day.

The commemoration of Yom Hazikaron begins at sundown

with a one-minute siren throughout the country, during which the nation comes to a standstill. Traffic halts, pedestrians stop in their tracks, and the entire country shares collective remembrance for that brief moment. The siren marks the beginning of the official ceremonies held at the Western Wall in Yerushalayim and military cemeteries across the country.

The following day, a two-minute siren at 11 a.m. signals the start of the prominent memorial ceremonies.

During Yom Hazikaron, the stories of the fallen are brought to the forefront. Media outlets dedicate their programming to documentaries, interviews, and stories about the lives of the soldiers and victims of terrorism. This collective storytelling serves as a tribute and a means of communal mourning and remembrance. It's a way for society to engage with the personal stories behind the statistics, bringing a human face to the losses endured.

Special assemblies and programs are held in schools, often including visits from military representatives or family members of the fallen. These programs aim to educate the younger generation about the sacrifices made for their country and to instil a sense of national pride and responsibility. The stories of bravery, courage, and sacrifice become part of the national narrative, shaping the values and identity of future generations.

The impact of Yom Hazikaron extends beyond the Jewish majority, as it includes remembering the sacrifices made by all of Israel's citizens, including Druze and Bedouin soldiers who have served in the Israeli Defense Forces. The Druze are a monotheistic religious and ethnic group known for their unique religious beliefs, originating in the Near

East. The Bedouins are a traditionally nomadic Arab ethnic group known for their desert-dwelling lifestyle and rich cultural traditions. This inclusivity reflects Israeli society's complex and diverse nature and the shared burden of defence and loss.

Yom Hazikaron is also a day highlighting the ongoing conflicts and security challenges Israel faces. Each year, new names are added to the list of the fallen, a sad reminder that the price of freedom and security is ongoing. The day reflects on the cost of conflict and the yearning for peace, with many Israelis hoping for a future where such sacrifices will no longer be necessary.

The transition from Yom Hazikaron to Yom Ha'atzmaut is a powerful and emotional shift. As the sun sets and Yom Hazikaron comes to a close, the country's mood changes dramatically. The solemnity and mourning of Memorial Day give way to the celebrations of Independence Day, with fireworks, parties, and festive events. This transition embodies the resilience and spirit of the Israeli people, acknowledging the pain of the past while embracing the hope and joy of the future.

In conclusion, Yom Hazikaron is not just a day on the Israeli calendar but an expression of national identity, collective memory, and communal mourning. It reflects the deep scars of wars and conflicts, the sacrifices made for independence and survival, and the resilience of a nation that has faced immense challenges since its inception.

As Israel continues to navigate its complex geopolitical landscape, Yom Hazikaron remains a vital component of its national fabric, a day of remembrance, reflection, and respect for those who have given their lives for the country's existence and security.

"The State of Israel will not be established without the sword and the shadow of death will not leave the State of Israel." David Ben-Gurion, Israel's first Prime Minister.

"Every man and woman who fought and died for the State of Israel is a hero whose memory we honour not only on Memorial Day, but every day." Shimon Peres, former President and Prime Minister of Israel.

These quotes reflect the deep respect and gratitude felt towards those who have sacrificed for Israel's security and existence.

Chapter 14.

Yom Yerushalayim.

A City Reunited: A Tale of Triumph and Transformation.

Yom Yerushalayim, or Yerushalayim Day, is a significant and emotive day in the Israeli calendar, symbolising the reunification of Yerushalayim and its re-establishment as Israel's capital. Its celebration marks a moment of both historical and spiritual magnitude, resonating deeply within the Jewish community and beyond.

This chapter delves into Yom Yerushalayim's essence, origins, historical context, and how it is commemorated. It also reflects on its broader implications and relevance in today's world.

The origins of Yom Yerushalayim date back to the Six-Day War in June 1967, a conflict that dramatically altered the Middle East's geopolitical landscape. Following years of mounting tension and hostile acts from neighbouring countries, Israel launched preemptive strikes against Egypt, Jordan, and Syria.

The war resulted in a swift and decisive victory for Israel, with significant territorial gains. Among these was the capture of East Yerushalayim, including the Old City, from Jordanian control.

Yerushalayim, a city steeped in thousands of years of history, holds immense religious and cultural significance. For Jews, the city is the heart of their ancient homeland, the site of the First and Second Temples, and the focus of Jewish prayer for centuries. The Western Wall, a remnant of the Second Temple, symbolises Jewish perseverance and faith.

For Christians, Yerushalayim is where Yeshua lived, preached, and was crucified, making it a focal point of Christian pilgrimage. Muslims revere the city as the location of the Al-Aqsa Mosque and the Dome of the Rock, where Prophet Muhammad is believed to have ascended.

The reunification of Yerushalayim in 1967 was a moment of profound joy and relief for many Jews worldwide. It ended 19 years of Jordanian control over the Old City, during which Jews were denied access to their holiest sites.

In contrast, the Israeli government implemented a religious freedom policy, allowing access to sacred places for all faiths. This reunification's emotional and spiritual impact cannot be overstated, as it represented a military victory and a restoration of historical and religious connections.

Yom Yerushalayim was established in 1968 by the Israeli government to commemorate this momentous event. Celebrated on the 28th day of the Hebrew month of Iyar, the day corresponds to the date the Old City was captured. It is a national holiday in Israel, marked by various events and ceremonies.

The day typically features state ceremonies, memorial services for soldiers who died in the Six-Day War, and festive parades and gatherings. Educational programs in schools focus on the historical and cultural significance of Yerushalayim, and religious services in synagogues include special prayers of thanksgiving.

One of the most notable events of Yom Yerushalayim is the Rikudgalim, or Flag Dance, where thousands of people, mainly religious Zionist youth, march through the streets of Yerushalayim, waving Israeli flags and singing patriotic songs.

The march culminates at the Western Wall, where participants gather for prayers and celebrations. While a display of national pride and joy for many, this event is also a source of tension and controversy, particularly as the route often passes through predominantly Arab neighbourhoods in East Yerushalayim.

The commemoration of Yom Yerushalayim is not without its complexities and controversies. For Palestinians and many in the Arab world, the Israeli capture of East Yerushalayim in 1967 is viewed as the beginning of an ongoing occupation.

The day is a reminder of displacement, loss, and the unresolved status of Yerushalayim, a city claimed as a capital by both Israelis and Palestinians. The political and religious sensitivities surrounding Yerushalayim make Yom Yerushalayim a focal point of debate and differing perspectives.

Yom Yerushalayim has evolved to encompass a broader range of observances and interpretations in recent years. Some Israelis, particularly those on the political left, use the day to advocate for peace and coexistence, holding events that emphasise the city's diversity and the need for a just resolution to the Israeli-Palestinian conflict. Others focus on Yerushalayim's spiritual and historical aspects, exploring its rich cultural heritage and significance to different faiths.

The day also raises questions about the nature of national memory and the role of commemoration in shaping a society's identity. Yom Yerushalayim is not just a remembrance of a historical event; it reflects how Israelis see themselves and their place in the world. It is a celebration of resilience and survival and a reminder of ongoing conflicts and the challenges of achieving lasting peace.

In conclusion, Yom Yerushalayim is a day of profound significance, encapsulating a complex tapestry of history, religion, emotion, and politics. It commemorates a pivotal moment in Israel's history while highlighting the enduring challenges and sensitivities surrounding Yerushalayim.

The day serves as a reminder of the city's unique place in the hearts and minds of people worldwide and the importance of striving for a future where Yerushalayim can be a symbol of peace and unity rather than division and conflict. As the city evolves and its story unfolds, Yom Yerushalayim will remain a focal point for reflection, celebration, and contemplation, not just for Israelis but all who cherish Yerushalayim's rich legacy.

Chapter 15.

What have we learned?

Some common themes.

The non-Scriptural festivals we've covered in this book are a diverse representation of the Jewish calendar, each with unique historical, cultural, and religious significance. While finding a common link among these festivals may seem challenging, they collectively reflect essential Jewish people and faith aspects. In examining these holidays, we can identify several overarching lessons and themes that shed light on Jewish identity and values.

Many of these festivals commemorate moments in Jewish history marked by adversity, persecution, or challenges. For instance, Tisha B'Av mourns the destruction of the First and Second Temples. At the same time, Yom HaShoah is a solemn day to remember the Holocaust. Despite these tragic events, Jewish people have shown remarkable resilience in preserving their faith, culture, and community.

Several festivals celebrate the idea of redemption and deliverance. Purim, for instance, commemorates the salvation of the Jewish people from Haman's plot to exterminate them. Hanukkah commemorates the oil miracle and the Second Temple's rededication. These stories emphasise that hope and salvation are possible even in despair.

Many Jewish festivals are tied to the Land of Israel. Tu Bishvat, for example, is known as the "New Year for Trees" and underscores the deep connection between the Jewish people and the land they have historically inhabited. Yom

Ha'atzmaut and Yom Yerushalayim celebrate the State of Israel's establishment and the Yerushalayim reunification, further emphasising this connection.

Festivals like Lag BaOmer and Tzom Tammuz encourage spiritual reflection, renewal, and growth. Lag BaOmer, for instance, is associated with the teachings of Rabbi Shimon bar Yochai and represents a period of increased spiritual study and development. Tzom Tammuz is a fast day that encourages introspection and repentance.

Many Jewish holidays emphasise the importance of community and unity among the Jewish people. Purim involves giving gifts to one another and sharing a festive meal. These customs reinforce the idea that Jews are part of a larger community, and their actions affect one another.

Yom HaShoah, or Holocaust Remembrance Day, serves as a solemn reminder of the atrocities of the Holocaust. It underscores the importance of remembering history, bearing witness, and learning from past horrors to prevent their repetition. This commitment to remembrance is a significant aspect of Jewish identity.

Yom HaAliyah, Yom Ha'atzmaut, and Yom Yerushalayim celebrate aspects of Jewish national identity and sovereignty. Yom HaAliyah marks the contributions of immigrants to Israel, Yom Ha'atzmaut celebrates the establishment of the State of Israel, and Yom Yerushalayim marks the reunification of Yerushalayim. These holidays reflect the modern Jewish nation's desire for self-determination and independence.

In conclusion, while these non-Scriptural festivals I've covered may appear diverse in their themes and historical contexts, they offer valuable insights into the Jewish people and faith. These celebrations highlight the resilience, faith, and enduring connection to the Land of Israel. They also underscore the importance of community, spirituality, and learning from history. Ultimately, these festivals serve as a testament to the rich tapestry of Jewish identity and the enduring values that have sustained the Jewish people throughout their history.

Chapter 16.

This is not the end. It's merely the beginning.

In the journey through the pages of "God's Tapestry of Time," we have explored the rich tapestry of Jewish feasts, fasts, and festivals. This book has delved into Scriptural and non-Scriptural observances, seeking to unveil the intricate threads that bind the Jewish people to their traditions, faith, and the Divine.

As we end this enlightening journey, it is crucial to reflect on the significance and enduring relevance of these celebrations in the lives of the Jewish community and how they should also impact our lives as we respond to God's commandments and His long and faithful interaction with His people.

Scriptural Jewish feasts, fasts and festivals, Shabbat, Rosh Chodesh, Pesach, HaMatzot, HaBikkurim, Shavuot, Yom Teruah, Yom Kippur, and Sukkot, we have seen how they serve as cornerstones of Jewish religious life. They are historical commemorations and testimonies to the enduring covenant between the Jewish people and the God of Israel.

Passover, for example, reminds us of the Exodus from Egypt, symbolising liberation from oppression. Shavuot marks the giving of the Torah on Mount Sinai, emphasising the importance of God's commandments in Jewish life. Sukkot encourages gratitude for the abundance of nature, and Yom Kippur offers a chance for self-reflection and repentance. These Scriptural feasts serve as spiritual anchors, grounding the Jewish community in its heritage and providing a sense of continuity and identity.

In contrast, non-Scriptural Jewish festivals like Hanukkah and Purim may not be explicitly mentioned in the Torah but are highly significant. Hanukkah, for instance, commemorates the story of the miracle of the oil in the temple and highlights the resilience of the Jewish people in the face of adversity.

On the other hand, Purim celebrates the victory over Haman's evil plot, emphasising the theme of divine providence. These festivals showcase the adaptability and creativity of Jewish tradition as it has responded to new challenges and circumstances throughout history.

The diversity of Jewish celebrations is a testament to the multifaceted nature of Jewish identity. While the Scriptural feasts are deeply rooted in religious commandments, non-Scriptural festivals often evolve in response to historical events or local customs. Together, they form a mosaic that reflects the complex and ever-evolving identity of the Jewish people.

These celebrations also foster community and belonging among Jewish individuals and families. They are occasions for coming together, sharing meals, and reinforcing bonds. The Seder table at Pesach, the lighting of the Hanukkiah during Hanukkah, and the raucous festivities of Purim are all opportunities for connection and unity. They bridge generations, passing down traditions and values from one to another.

Moreover, Jewish feasts, fasts, and festivals hold universal lessons that extend beyond the boundaries of the Jewish community. Freedom, justice, resilience, and faith resonate with people of all backgrounds. The Passover story of liberation inspires those who seek freedom from oppression. The lessons of Yom Kippur, with its focus on repentance and forgiveness, are relevant to anyone who seeks personal growth and reconciliation. In this way, these traditions bridge different cultures and faiths, promoting understanding and empathy.

In conclusion, "God's Tapestry of Time" has offered a deep dive into the world of Jewish feasts, fasts, and festivals, showcasing their spiritual significance, cultural richness, and enduring relevance. Whether Scriptural or non-Scriptural, these celebrations are historical relics and living traditions that connect generations, strengthen community bonds, and convey timeless messages of hope, resilience, and faith.

They are threads in the tapestry of human history, reminding us of our shared values and the enduring power of faith and tradition in our lives.

Printed in Great Britain
by Amazon